| The Heart of Listening

Other titles in the School of Psychotherapy and Counselling (SPC) Series of Regent's College:

Wise Therapy: Philosophy for Counsellors   Tim Le Bon
Embodied Theories   Ernesto Spinelli and Sue Marshall (eds)

SPC SERIES

The Heart of Listening

Attentional Qualities in Psychotherapy

Rosalind Pearmain

CONTINUUM
London and New York

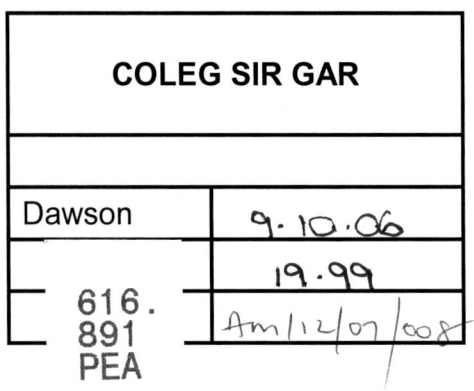

Continuum
The Tower Building
11 York Road
London SE1 7NX

370 Lexington Avenue
New York
NY 10017–6503

www.continuumbooks.com

© 2001 Rosalind Pearmain

All rights reserved. No part of this publication may be reproduced or transmitted in any form or by any means, electronic or mechanical, including photocopying, recording or any information storage or retrieval system, without prior permission in writing from the publishers.

First published 2001

British Library Cataloguing-in-Publication Data
A catalogue record for this book is available from the British Library.

ISBN 0–8264–5195–0 (paperback)
       0–8264–5783–5 (hardback)

Designed and typeset by Kenneth Burnley, Wirral, Cheshire.
Printed and bound in Great Britain by Biddles Ltd, Guildford and King's Lynn.

Contents

General Introduction to The SPC Series vii
Preface: Origins xi

Introduction 1
1 Dancing on a Pin-head – Naming the In-Between 12
2 Knowing and Feeling – How Do We Know What We Know? 39
3 The Art of Attending – Meditation and Psychotherapy 59
4 The Heart as Listener 73
5 Attunement: A Relational Sense of Focused Awareness 92
6 Amplification: A Relational Sense of Spaciousness 109
7 Going Deeper: Reverberation and Depth 119
Conclusion 126

Notes 131
Further Sources 140
Index 141

Know Deeply, Know Thyself More Deeply

Go deeper than love, for the soul has greater depths,
Love is like the grass, but the heart is deep wild rock
Molten, yet dense and permanent.
Go down to your deep old heart, and lose sight of yourself.
And lose sight of me whom you turbulently loved.
Let us lose sight of ourselves, and break the mirrors.
For the fierce curve of our lives is moving again to the depths
Out of sight, in the deep living heart.[1]

General Introduction to The SPC Series

IT IS BOTH A GREAT HONOUR AND A PLEASURE to welcome readers to The SPC Series.

The School of Psychotherapy and Counselling at Regent's College (SPC) is one of the largest and most widely respected psychotherapy, counselling and counselling psychology training institutes in the UK. The SPC Series published by Continuum marks a major development in the School's mission to initiate and develop novel perspectives centred upon the major topics of debate within the therapeutic professions so that their impact and influence upon the wider social community may be more adequately understood and assessed.

A brief overview of SPC

Although its origins lie in an innovative study programme developed by Antioch University, USA in 1977, SPC has been in existence in its current form since 1990. SPC's MA in Psychotherapy and Counselling Programme obtained British validation with City University in 1991. More recently, the MA in Existential Counselling Psychology obtained accreditation from the British Psychological Society. SPC was also the first UK institute to develop a research-based MPhil/PhD Programme in Psychotherapy and Counselling, and this has been validated by City University since 1992. Largely on the impetus of its first Dean, Emmy van Deurzen, SPC became a full training and accrediting member of the United Kingdom Council for Psychotherapy (UKCP) and continues to maintain a strong and active presence in that organization through its Professional Members, many of whom also hold professional affiliations with the British Psychological Society (BPS), the British Association of Counselling and Psychotherapy (BACP), the Society for Existential Analysis (SEA) and the European Society for Communicative Psychotherapy (ESCP).

SPC's other programmes include: a Foundation Certificate in Psychotherapy and Counselling, Advanced Professional Diploma Programmes in Existential Psychotherapy and Integrative Psychotherapy, and a series of intensive Continuing Professional Development and related adjunct courses such as its innovative Legal and Family Mediation Programmes.

With the personal support of the President of Regent's College, Mrs Gillian Payne, SPC has recently established the Psychotherapy and Counselling Consultation Centre housed on the college campus which provides individual and group therapy for both private individuals and organizations.

As a unique centre for learning and professional training, SPC has consistently emphasized the comparative study of psychotherapeutic theories and techniques while paying careful and accurate attention to the philosophical assumptions underlying the theories being considered and the philosophical coherence of those theories to their practice-based standards and professional applications within a diversity of private and public settings. In particular, SPC fosters the development of faculty and graduates who think independently, are theoretically well informed and able skilfully and ethically to apply the methods of psychotherapy and counselling in practice, in the belief that knowledge advances through criticism and debate, rather than by uncritical adherence to received wisdom.

The integrative attitude of SPC

The underlying ethos upon which the whole of SPC's educational and training programme rests is its *integrative attitude*, which can be summarized as follows.

There exists a multitude of perspectives in current psychotherapeutic thought and practice, each of which expresses a particular philosophical viewpoint on an aspect of being human. No one single perspective or set of underlying values and assumptions is universally shared.

Given that a singular, or shared, view does not exist, SPC seeks to enable a learning environment which allows competing and diverse models to be considered both conceptually and experientially so that their areas of interface and divergence can be exposed, considered and clarified. This aim espouses the value of holding the tension between contrasting and often contradictory ideas, of 'playing with' their experiential possibilities and of allowing a paradoxical security which can 'live with' and at times even thrive in the absence of final and fixed truths.

SPC defines this aim as 'the integrative attitude' and has designed all of its courses so that its presence will challenge and stimulate all aspects of our students' and trainees' learning experience. SPC believes that this deliberate engagement with difference should be reflected in the manner in which the faculty relate to students, clients and colleagues at all levels. In such a way this attitude may be seen as the lived expression of the foundational ethos of SPC.

The SPC Series

The series evolved out of a number of highly encouraging and productive discussions between the Publishing Director at Continuum Books, Mr Robin Baird-Smith, and the present Academic Dean of SPC, Professor Ernesto Spinelli.

From the start, it was recognized that SPC, through its faculty and Professional Members, was in a unique position to provide a series of wide-ranging, accessible and pertinent texts intended to challenge, inspire and influence debate in a variety of issues and areas central to therapeutic enquiry. Further, SPC's focus and concern surrounding the ever more pervasive impact of therapeutic ideas and practices upon all sections of contemporary society highlighted the worth, if not necessity, of a series that could address key topics from an informed, critical and non-doctrinal perspective.

The publication of the first three texts in the SPC Series during 2001 marks the beginning of what is hoped will be a long and fruitful relationship between SPC and Continuum. More than that, there exists the hope that the series will become identified by professionals and public alike as an invaluable contributor to the advancement of psychotherapy and counselling as a vigorously self-critical, socially minded and humane profession.

PROFESSOR ERNESTO SPINELLI
Series Editor

Preface: Origins

FOR MORE THAN TWENTY YEARS I have been practising a form of meditation called Sahaj Marg (natural or simple way).[1] It is a modern form of the ancient and classical system Raj Yoga. The focus of meditation is on the supposition that divine light is in the heart. In this system there is a direct transmission of pranahuti (divine essence) to the heart. When attention is gathered within the heart centre there is a somatic and affective quality of feeling. It is like a warm, soft, transparent substance that is neither water nor air. Sinking into it, my focus keeps dropping through the centre and I feel as if caught in a finer and finer sound or smoother and smoother feeling which brings lightness, expansion, qualities of feeling that are new, like a kind of taste, or meaning, or very deep longing, of love or enormous and infinite space.

The process is never the same each time. There is a search for the profoundest sense of self within and this keeps deepening and deepening. Sometimes a feeling of connection and absolute absorption comes. At other times there is just longing and waiting. Sometimes there are just thoughts about things to do and phone calls to be made. Yet, despite the undulations of living through time, the manner of perceiving and experiencing keeps getting more subtle, more about qualities than forms, almost invisible or untastable but more and more profound in meaning. It is an experience that gives a sense of lightness and transcendence but the process of a spiritual path always evokes difficult emotional, psychological and existential challenges.

Experiences are one thing but the purpose of the meditation practice is not to simply explore the beauty and awesomeness of transcendental landscapes. It is to bring something that is tasted as a quality and meaning into everyday life. Over the years, the biggest change is that the way I perceive people comes increasingly from a more feeling-centred, or heart-centred perspective. This is not the same as being emotional or sentimental or even irrational. It is simply a closer sense of belonging to the human race.

As part of a doctoral research project I interviewed more than thirty meditators from all over the world with many different occupations: bankers, teachers, business people, artists, craftsmen, therapists, film-makers, social workers, musicians. The initial plan of the interviews was semi-structured and was focused on the meditation experience and changes they had noticed. What happened was that unexpectedly most of the interviewees started telling me about their sense of the heart. What was even more disconcerting was that there were so many different ways of describing its meaning – from the most sublime metaphysical notions of akasha, of space, of the divine ground of being, to a kind of orientation, or empathic capacity. None of these different conceptions can be aggregated into any neat conception or construct that can be understood by intellect.

There follow some extracts from these responses:

> The heart is sort of occupied with feeling the pain in other people's hearts. The heart is the thing in you that is drawn to comfort the needs of other human beings.

> The heart is the base of any action. Or any thought. That's it ... It is the thread.

> One consults the heart and I feel the real knowledge is contained within the heart, it is something higher than the intellect, and if one consults the heart I feel that it is more knowledgeable.

> The heart is the most important thing we have here, because if we think and approach a person with our head, it's a mental approach, but if we approach with our heart, it's a real approach, because the heart is really what makes us understand.
>
> I think some kind of scanning. There's not much research gone into that...I can feel it is more important for example when I teach, to let the thoughts grow out from the heart. All people know what it means when we say this man is doing a heartfelt thing, it is a real thing.
>
> I understood nothing of what it was before...when I did my medical studies I saw when people had an arteriography of their coronary arteries and when they got this probe in the heart, I saw people feeling something strange, they were as if they were going to die, without something happening on the screen with rhythm or blood pressure, they would describe it as a very strange and astonishing feeling, so it reminded me of these sayings about it being the centre of the person.... Through this practice of meditation...I try to relate at heart level because it facilitates so much contact, preventing resistances, competition, aggressivity, all these kinds of human conditions. So the heart has become something experienced.
>
> The heart is related to feeling obviously, the heart sense is being the compass.
>
> If the heart would be developed in human beings, the way of life would be very different.

This research opened a whole new vista of enquiry to me; it has been a source of wondering further about the role of feeling (heart) and thought in psychotherapy. It bothers me that a heart element is so much lacking in the field of psychotherapy dominated by intellectual or technical attitudes towards humanness. Without imposing spiritual philosophies or dogmas on anyone, it seems increasingly important to restore at least the basic value of sentience, feeling and fellow feeling to our understanding of relationship and the possibilities of living together more harmoniously. These special moments of connection are felt to be the most valued in human encounters and have also been identified as vital to therapeutic change.

As a therapist, I have noticed it is these deepest, heart-based feelings that provide most meaning and ground to the work.

For the sake of protecting privacy and confidentiality, all identifying information has been altered in every case example and session vignettes throughout the book. For the same reason, many of the examples are actually composites of several persons.

Dedicated to Revered Parthasarathi Rajagopalachari

For Alan, Erica and Daniel

Introduction

'My head is getting bigger, but my heart is shrinking' (trainee psychotherapist from Japan).

I AM SITTING OPPOSITE A WOMAN in her fifties in my small consulting room and study. We are both ensconced in Ikea chairs and there is a white rug connecting the floor where our feet rest. In a low voice, she is relaying to me a stream of unspeakable cruelties and deprivations visited on her from earliest childhood from individuals supported by religious institutions. The textural details and atmosphere are vivid and pungent. It is a daily misery of different kinds of terrifying anticipations and unremitting real events in wretched physical squalour. There is a disorientating combination of horror and ordinariness.

How and why on earth can I sit there listening? Feeling? Not saying much at all? Does it even help that I am sitting there? That is the only clear thing I know. It does help. It would not help perhaps if she were to go on telling me similar things for ever. Nor perhaps would it serve a purpose if she decided not to tell me at all. At this moment, it is just being willing to stay in the room and hear her.

Something is hurting in my chest. I feel as if a spade is digging out a cavity, something very deep is stirred, moved. I need to breathe and let go so that the space can keep getting opened and receiving. She is telling me things that I can only receive at the profoundest level possible within me. It does not have a name or form but it is where I mean something to myself. Afterwards, alone, I have to cry, but the tears come from the same meaning place where I am crying for her, for me, for us, for all human beings.

All I have to offer is attention, feeling and some kind of capacity to resonate with her. This is it. Theories can assist me in accessing the inner buried stories behind the surface and in this way can help me to feel more or resonate. Yet sometimes theories get in the way and cover over these responses because they are too abstracted from the live moment.

Research continues to emphasize the central role of the relationship in psychotherapy in contributing to valued outcomes. Thus it can be imagined that psychotherapy is about the art of human relationship. Yet this is often obscured by theories that distance us from our own humanity. What I have found moving about the material gleaned from other authors in this book is a reminder of the delicacy and complexity of sentience we possess for relationship. This capacity can be developed further largely, I would suggest, by deepening our capacity for fellow feeling or heart connection.

I once had the good fortune to observe my spiritual teacher (Parthasarathi Rajagopalachari) meeting with a large group of people. These people came from a wide range of backgrounds, languages, education and occupations. I watched how he responded to each person who approached him. He seemed to meet them effortlessly, without resistance, and to engage in specific and novel ways with each person such that the person truly felt met and heard and valued and enjoyed. This was an expression of a developed human heart that so many facets and qualities could be attuned to and played with warmth and humour. This was an inspiration for the possibilities of humanness and the infinite space within the heart.

This book explores these three dimensions of attention, feeling and resonance through three main sources: the conception of heart as a way of perception or feeling from the perennial philosophies and mystical traditions. It draws on the field of infant observation to illustrate more vividly the exquisite human responsiveness that is intrinsic to relating, and on current approaches to perception and consciousness that are more radical in uniting mind and feeling together. Finally, the book examines three modalities of attending such that heart listening can be enhanced. Although arising from very different empirical sources, each of these areas of understanding can inform us about what is happening when we listen to someone and how we can go more towards our humanness or come towards others from our heart.

What happens when we meet?

It is in the smallest ways that we demonstrate our best (and worst) capacities as human beings in how we relate to each other. These may be minuscule qualities of touch, slight shifts of expression, and a subtle moderation in tone of voice. When people are most caring and intimate, these tiny movements speak of enormous feeling and meaning. Even in mundane moments, this exquisite sensitivity is being played out and its impact can be enormous. Yet human contact is our main source of sustainment even when it is transacted in a far more cursory and automatic way, even when we have to watch soap operas to see the same clichéd rhythms of meeting and passing in contrived story-lines.

How many meetings occur each day? So many times we greet and exchange and then pass on. On each occasion, something of that meeting stays with us like a kind of taste which flavours the next encounter or the sense of the day. If we walk around our neighbourhood and meet people we know, it feels a very different experience from when we meet nobody. It is so ordinary that we take it for granted. Words like 'having a conversation with somebody', 'having a relationship', 'bumping into someone', are strangely remote from the powerful inner experiences we go through during such contacts. Inside, enormous variations of response go on: hearts beat faster, muscles contract or relax, we feel warm, numb, more alive, more full or empty, light or heavy. In short, if we were alert, we might notice complex and different combinations in response to every person we meet. Eugene Gendlin[1] in his teaching of the 'felt sense' of things asks people to allow a felt sense of a person to come. For each person it will be different. We can get a felt sense of someone even when we do not remember their name or who they are. Bodily and viscerally, the responses and reactions that go on within each small moment of relating are multidimensional. They are also felt by others whom we meet but often out of conscious awareness.

At the present time, the emerging disciplines of infant development studies, consciousness studies, neuroscience and cognitive psychology are offering increasing emphasis on the feeling level of knowing. When we stress the crucial importance of the therapeutic relationship we are faced with a challenge of working with the unseen and the felt and the heard rather than what is seen. Whereas we have many maps and images of a separate person, of internal organs or brain, of an individual's style of being, of her voice or the various roles she may play in life, imagining a relationship is usually more abstract. Being in a relationship is something that is felt rather than seen.

The work of Daniel Stern and other infant researchers

How then can these inner subjective experiences be known to others?

In the 1980s, Daniel Stern[2] as an infant psychiatrist was confronted with two apparently incompatible sets of knowledge about the infant. One came from the inferred infant of psychoanalysis. The other was emerging from a body of new research about the capacities and responses of infants from birth. In drawing these together, Stern created a new model of infant development. Within this model a sense of self was apparent in many patternings and responses expressed non-verbally and expressively from birth and did not depend on language. Stern has argued that the infant does not begin in autism; instead the baby unfolds through different levels of intersubjectivity. Stern needed to find terms that could describe the motor, sensory and affective presence and communications from babies. He used terms from Gestalt psychologists and aesthetics to describe the surging, flowing phrasings and subtle processes of attunement between carer and infant. Recently, he has redefined these phrases of response and activity as *vitality contours*.[3] Such vitality contours are the real time moments of experiencing. Within relationships we embody these in numerous ways in movements and speech and narrative forms – beginnings, middles and endings have a shape and form. This is a dynamic image of process that is very helpful in articulating the units of experience prior to language or conceptualization. For psychotherapy this work gives us tools to name what has been unnamed or has been designated as ineffable.

What is shown about the process of relating?

The work of Stern,[2,3,4] Trevarthen[5,6] and others in the same field provides us with vivid descriptions and analyses of early processes of relating that are repeated in different forms as adults. As such they provide a valuable reference for considering the shapes of contact and shift that occur in small moments of interaction. These are presented in Chapter 1 and related to the psychotherapeutic relationship. There are central elements emerging within Stern and Trevarthen's notions of relationship and intersubjectivity.[1] Relationship in its earliest forms seems to require a kind of echo and resonance with what is communicated from the other. A balance between what is like me and what is different is the most interesting and enlivening counterpoint to the tune of each person. Think, for instance, of the first conversation between two lovers.

Feeling known and knowing myself through the other's response requires making something up as we go along. What seems to help the continuing going along is sufficient accuracy in reflection – so that I recognize someone is joining in with me.

What also seems to help is the way this may be expanded and played with so that it changes and moves somewhere slightly different.

Then, with each small exchange of phrasing or melody, something else comes into being. This is like a summation of all of these pieces together with the possibility of many more. Each of our meetings becomes a pattern for meeting itself: the meaning of meeting, the meaning of being someone who can meet another, the promise and the perils that arise in all of it.

The beauty of all of this is that most of this happens anyway. It happens because we appear to have the capacity to be extraordinarily sensitive to how others are from moment to moment. Too much theoretical knowledge can obscure the obvious. It can also hide the level of refined sentience and feeling that exists in our humanness.

Perceiving, feeling and knowing

How do concepts mutate into relational processes? How do we know what we know? How does 'knowing about' translate into knowing you? The field of psychotherapy is not short of theories or conceptualizations, but it is perhaps not 'long' enough on how these understandings may be used in our meetings with others in therapy. What has always been most extraordinary to observe in working as a therapist are the sinews and tissues of perception and attention, the focus of intention and feeling, the places of experience prior to category or theory. Since each moment is so utterly dependent on our perceptual processes, which in turn are rooted in our bodied experiencing, it is surprising that so little attention has been directed to these primary areas of orientation. However, we are now at a time when there are interesting paths of convergence and coalescence arising from related disciplines that can facilitate our understanding of the subtleties of relationship, intersubjectivity, perception and thought.

In Chapter 2, some attention is given to these questions

through various perspectives including James Gibson,[7] a cognitive psychologist who was interested in developing an ecological view of perception as a kind of perception in action. Some time is spent also in considering the new theories of Antonio Damasio,[8,9] a neuroscientist who has examined the relation of feeling to consciousness and the sense of self in knowing. In this chapter, there are more links made between feeling and perceiving and how the basis of consciousness is feeling or sentience, and that is a primary basis for our relation with others. Damasio's work with neurologically impaired patients shows that we can know and recognize others as friends or enemies through feeling, even if we do not know their names or occupations. There are many interesting implications for this in our understanding of what consciousness is, and how we respond in our awareness to our clients.

Meditation and psychotherapy

If relationship processes are implicit and out of conscious awareness, to what extent can we be conscious or intentional with them? Can we consciously focus awareness in order to attend better? In Chapter 3, the value of meditation as attentional training is considered in relation to the art of psychotherapy.

Some psychotherapy practitioners who are practising meditation have consistently reported how this enhances their work (Epstein,[10] Welwood,[11] Speeth,[12] Coltart,[13] Kornfield,[14] and Brandon[15]). They find a capacity to attend to others which seems to offer more of the things that are recognized as useful or necessary for therapists. For example, they have reported a greater capacity to be open and aware; a capacity to tolerate the unknown, to be vulnerable, to sit with very painful images and experiences, to support their clients in the midst of extreme feeling or profound insecurity. Attention itself can be strengthened in its concentration or focus or in its acceptance of all that arises in consciousness. Even when psychotherapists do not practise meditation they have to learn to listen and attend for long periods of time without losing concentration or focus. Clients appear to notice consistency of attention acutely and are conscious of when it slips away or glazes over. The reciprocal impact of attention is not an area that has received so much reflection in psychotherapy. Attention itself creates a certain kind of field of possibility. Most therapists will be familiar with how even very small changes in state and feeling can affect the therapeutic process in very subtle ways for better or worse. Some quality in our attention is communicated to our clients. The role of meditation and attention in psychotherapy is further explored in Chapter 3 to show that attention is a neglected but central aspect of psychotherapeutic process.

What is the heart and its relation to feeling and listening?

Having explored how relating requires a capacity to be attuned to others and to our own awareness, Chapter 4 addresses the key issue of the heart. It looks at feeling as the basis of thought and knowing. It suggests that particular ways of integrating attention and feeling may be useful in our work as psychotherapists. These ways are derived from meditational practice. However, they differ in a crucial way. They are based on a relational rather than private inner focus. Such a relational sense is linked with feeling and what some would call heart. The best metaphor for this is music and the role of musical instruments in expressing and communicating music. As therapists we can discover how we attune to, amplify and deepen the sounds we hear. We may intend to truly respond to others and to allow more improvisation and meaning to arise from a profound capacity to listen and to resonate with them.

The aim in this book is to reclaim an experiential level of knowledge. It requires undoing the shorthand, specific dictionary meaning for the deeper, open, wider and different base of experience that can support a whole continent using the same word. For me experiencing is linked with feeling and heart. However, both of those terms are ambiguous. Feeling can mean emotion, it can mean something more vague and diffuse, like sensing. In some languages there is no separation between feeling and emotion.

The word 'heart' has a poetic or romantic connotation; it can also mean something concrete or something metaphysical. For the purposes of this book, it is possible to read the word 'heart' and to respond to its meaning at any of these levels, expressive, metaphorical, concrete, mystical. At the very least, in current discourse, heart continues to have a charged meaning and to represent something very significant within human existence. At the very most, the heart is perceived as a central link between the divine and the human and the basis of mind and perception. Feeling and emotion have often been seen as opposite to thought and rationality. I hope to show that they are an intrinsic part of both.

In Chapter 4, the conceptions of heart in perennial philosophies (especially in Sufism and Raj Yoga) are described as well as more contemporary research on the heart. This leads to the consideration of how heart listening can be developed further. The book draws on the perennial philosophy of Raj Yoga and Sufism rather than Buddhist approaches which have more often been referred to in the context of psychotherapy (Epstein,[10] Kornfield,[14] Welwood,[11] Crook and Fontana,[16]). The arrival place is an emphasis on heart or feeling in perception. I propose ways that we can attend to others from heart and feeling in order to re-cognize the basis of relation and connection in our knowing of each other.

The heart of listening – attunement, amplification and depth

Three dimensions of meditative types of attention may be linked with concentrative, mindful and Taoist meditational processes. However, I suggest that they also involve what

Almaas has described as essence or presence within us, or within the gathering of felt sense underlying spoken words and thoughts.[17] In this felt 'heart sense' we provide a kind of resonant place of hearing and feeling availability. I suggest that these three modalities of presence can be called attunement, amplification and depth that involves reverberation. This is what is meant by the heart of listening.

Over several years, during some courses and workshops with adults involved in counselling and psychotherapy, I have invited some exploration of the effects of different ways of intention in attention and presence on the experience of being and knowing the other. These small experiments appear to show very interesting distinctions between modalities of presence and what is picked up from others. These modalities are clarified in the final part of the book and some practical exercises are suggested to try them out.

Summary

In this book I am proposing a reawakening to the concrete ground of feeling or experiencing as something that is specific rather than intangible and therefore unreliable and discountable. I am drawing from different sources of understanding about the role of feeling in our sense of self, others and in a heart-based existence or presence. These sources are from both contemplative and scientific disciplines, from perennial and current perspectives.

I am inviting readers to consider the mysterious phenomenon of the heart in human development and consciousness. I am suggesting that it is possible to cultivate ways for attending that combine attentional aspects of meditational practice with the personal element of heart. Attention is not an abstract element of mind either. It is directed within the context of human presence in which others experience a texture and ambience that is personal and shifting from moment to moment.

Fundamentally, the art of psychotherapy is in weaving and

gathering threads of feeling and meaning from words into experiencing, from experiencing into words. The threads have to be fine and capable of unravelling or holding powerful feelings. The threads have to emerge out of an inchoate ground of repetitions, stucknesses, feelings and 'unthought knowns' which are glimpsed in many subtle ways. The threads are woven between both therapist and client. They spread from and to the world outside the room, but this is in a way less visible to view. Such threads form worlds of meaning.

For my client, with her terrible and haunting memories, these threads can potentially lead into the present with its different opportunities and meanings for her in this later phase of her life. There are no happy endings, no neat closures, but what has been imprisoning or shaming or isolating can change. In a small way, some barriers come down. It begins with one person in a room.

1 Dancing on a Pin-head – Naming the In-Between

'My mind is going Dave ...' (HAL – computer in Kubrick's film *2001*).

Definition of intersubjectivity: a deliberately sought sharing of experiences about events and things.[1]

There is a paradigm shift that is taking place in our thinking about who we are and how we know things. In the current debates about the nature of consciousness, there are those who would favour a view of consciousness closer to that portrayed by HAL the computer in *2001*. This view proposes that our brains are like computers which process information in an abstract form.

There are others who would argue that consciousness cannot be separated from embodiment or from an interrelational basis.[2] From this view, our mind is embedded within the whole nervous system and this nervous system is highly attuned to environment which includes others to the extent that we cannot make neat cut-off points between individual and world. Simplistically put, there is no brain without a body, there is no body without an environment, there is no sense of self or meaning without others to share it. We are indelibly interconnected with the world. This connection is mediated through our experiencing all the time whether or not we are conscious of this process.

What does all this have to do with psychotherapy? It means that our relational work involves highly developed capacities to attend to what has been pre-conscious or pre-attentive 'unthought knowns' or experiencings. We are working with implicit felt knowledge. We are working with micro-seconds of shift and movement and are learning continuously how to relate and make contact with others through our sameness and our difference. In thinking about the nature of this relating-focused work, we are fortunate to have access to a growing body of understanding about relationship as a highly sophisticated process which has been gathered from the field of infant observation studies.

Within the field of infant development, researchers demonstrate how the ways carers and infants relate to each other can determine physical, emotional and mental maturation. As therapists our work continues to embody this aspiration. Through the delicate work of making contact and sustaining relationships with clients, it is envisaged that capacities for new learning and new possibilities can become known to them.

This means a shift from how we used to consider the person as an island, surrounded by inaccessible waters of subjectivity. A predominant feature of the Cartesian view of human existence within the twentieth century has been of a separated individual locked into a fortress of self. Such a self can only be seen or known from the outside. Such a fortress was once mirrored in the stiff clothing and corsetry of the nineteenth century, and also in the complex vocabulary and syntax of speech. Subsequent cultural shifts have allowed restrictions in clothing to be steadily removed and styles of language and communication to change. In the movement to the present, the sense of the separateness of a human being has slowly evolved to one who is caught – intertwined inextricably with others.[3] This shift in substance and form is occurring at a level of geographical movement of peoples around the globe, at a massive communication level, at economic levels. More fundamentally, it is manifested in paradigm shifts in science, biology, systems theory, postmodern thought and in the growing emphasis on intersubjectivity as the locus of activity within psychotherapy.

Images of intersubjectivity from infant–carer observation

Among the most vivid ways we can actually see relationship is in filmed interactions of mothers and babies. What exactly do we see? From the outside, we see a baby inviting response from the mother; we see how she joins in, how there is a reciprocity of movement and echoes using gestures and expressions and sounds. Some kind of mutual dance comes into being with recognizable echoes of intensity, rhythm shape and form. When we see the dance we are reminded through resonance and bodily identification of the feelings that lead to movement. These feelings are the stuff of experiencing ourselves with others. They have to be described as qualities of movement and phrasing, of affect and shape. When we meet with persons in therapy we feel these qualities as background atmosphere, emotional temperature, sense of participation, and the open spaces and gaps between like vague and connecting strands of contact.

Example

Colwyn Trevarthen[4] describes very lyrically such sequences of communication. This is a summary of an example he describes between a mother and baby.

The baby has not long woken up. The mother gently approaches. Initially, she has to attune herself to the level of arousal or awareness of the infant so that her contact with the infant appears to slide into focus gradually rather than being experienced as a sudden explosion on to the scene. In a quiet, encouraging way, then, the mother matches the state of the infant and expresses it in words or touch or sounds. The baby responds by focusing on her face and becomes initially still as s/he orients towards her. Then the baby seems to express some kind of feeling: a facial expression, a sound, a wave of a hand or kicking movement. The mother then responds in a complementary way, such as smiling and joining with the infant in a similar rhythm or length of time. The infant then proceeds to attempt a more complex and focused kind of utterance.

These proto-conversations can be seen between six and twelve weeks and similar patterns have been observed in other cultures such as Africa and China. It has also been shown that mothers' tone and play of voice is pitched at the same level, using rhythmic and phrasing sequences across different languages – even in Chinese which is a tonal language. It has been observed that mother and infant become entrained within the same rhythmic and repetitive patterns during their exchanges. But it is important that the synchrony is never exactly matched or the experience of relation with another would not be felt.

Once the attention of the baby is engaged and the dialogue has begun, the analogy of a musical duet may be the best way to convey the unfolding sequence of relationship that may take place. This is sustained by moments of excitement-building and exchange between mother and infant which are signalled by the baby's smiles and sounds amplified and played back by the mother.

Consider this proto-conversation with how we begin when we meet new people or when we meet new clients. How do we start at the right level, provide some kind of encouragement, respond to what is given in a way that is both confirming and opening? All these moves are recognizable to us as adults because they seem so ordinary that they are out of our awareness or attention.

The role of imitation

A key capacity within this exchange is that of imitation; the baby can copy the mother's expression and sounds.[5] But by age two months the baby is apparently less likely to mirror isolated expressions. It is in fact the mother who tends to mimic more than the baby, but will more often respond by using a sound that conveys sympathetic attunement rather than absolute mimicry. It appears that babies prefer images of smiling, affectionate female faces.[9] The communication of smiling encouragement appears to help signal availability for relating to the infant.

The capacity for mimicry which was researched by Meltzoff and Moore[5] has challenged theories which would hold that some capacity for representation of experience would be needed for such a process. The immediate perceptive resonance and bodily attunement that appears in neonatal mimicry suggests a more primordial basis of perception through embodiment such that Merleau-Ponty has formulated.[6] Trevarthen calls this *readiness for response*, which allows the infant to re-present qualities or states of the other as experienced through body movement.[4] It has been shown that infants respond very differently to the more institutional or functional care that may be given by a nurse, which may result in passivity or withdrawal from the carer in contrast to the response to the mother. This suggests how specific affective and warmly invitational cues are communicated by the mother in a way that is not by institutional carers. In this respect, we have to surmise that the feelings of the mother are picked up by very subtle cues of movement phrasing, expression and so on. They would also resonate with previous known cues of voice and movement associated with the mother.

Communication with an older child

Allen Schore[7] is a neuroscientist and psychiatrist. He has written a ground-breaking work that elaborates the neurological development of infants which he links directly with the process of affective attunement with carers. It is the first time that this linking of physiology with relational processes has been correlated in this way. He cites another example of reunion between a mother and young child. The example describes a year-old child first observed in a room separate from its mother and then reunited with her. The child alone appears a little glum and directionless; his mode of being is flaccid and rather slow. When he sees his mother he crawls towards her slowly but with clear direction. He touches her arm. Her approach is gentle and moderated to be in the same kind of 'low-key' state of intensity as the baby. Her effect is to re-stimulate and arouse the child. She supports him while he kneels and he continues to stand and put his arm around her neck for more support. He smiles while doing this and he is then observed to look around the room with a 'sweet smile'.

'His expression gives the impression that he is quietly pleased with himself and with standing there.' He momentarily puts his thumb in his mouth and then turns towards her, pressing lightly into her body for a brief hug:

> The mother holds him for a few moments then puts him gently on the floor with a soft toy. Then in her moving away, after watching her for a few moments, he suddenly becomes energised and crawls towards the toy box and is very focused, and absorbed in play. (p. 101)[7]

This episode illustrates how the mother's relationship with her son has a kind of refuelling effect – a revitalizing reciprocity which enables closeness and separateness to be maintained while the child is able to be more mobile and exploratory. Schore calls this kind of behaviour 'synchronised bioenergetic transmissions'. Both infant and mother are initially highly focused on each other's faces which allows for a mutual regulatory system of arousal. This in turn creates a reaction – an energetic response to the arousal. Underlying this exchange is a deeper one of affective exchange. As an attachment behaviour, it allows for safety and pleasure and may trigger intense visual affective stimulation which will create interest – excitement – elation. As such it is a kind of entraining process. According to the *Oxford Dictionary* entrainment means *to cause to fall into synchronism with a rhythmic phenomenon*.

This whole sequence could be applied to many everyday kinds of interaction that we have as adults and that we have as psychotherapists. It is a kind of supportive response which people offer in the same kind of shape and form. We can think of how we attempt to 'cheer others up', or 'calm them down' if agitated. These relational exchanges encourage us to carry on – whether it is news that your football team has lost disastrously or that you have failed to get a job you wanted or that you are in touch with a sense of loss after a close family member has moved to Australia. Each different kind of event would evoke different levels of intensity in the cheering or calming process, but may have the same overall profile as a unit of movement, shape and form.

However, the studies from infant development allow us to appreciate the richness and dimensionality of relating process in slow action-replay. The two examples from infant development describe a series of parallel movements and responses occurring within a specific time period and unfolding within a particular sequence. They occur within a few seconds or minutes. Within them is contained a multitude of sensory-motor and affective processes and an overarching shape of phrasing similar to a melody or what Merleau-Ponty called an 'intentional arc'.[6] We are seeing how each person orientates towards each other – directly or more indirectly. We are seeing with what degrees of intensity the movements coincide or move forward. We are seeing small shifts in key and valency between one moment and another. Contact is made by touch, voice and eye contact. Contact may be begun in a more tentative way and then increase in intensity and fade away. The response to each movement may be resonated and expanded and subtly changed in form, shape or tone. There are movements in terms of widening and broadening contact, or more focused contact in one area. Different areas of body may be employed and different sensory modalities engaged with.

These nonverbal patterns of communication are simultaneously both affective and expressive through the dynamic flow patterns that are used – fast, slow, heavy, light, expansive, contracting, sustained, or quick changes. All of these convey emotional qualities as a synthesis of facial expression, sounds, gestures, movements, which are synchronized with the baby's. As such these behaviours could be termed 'emotional narratives': they convey meanings which are shared and of how motivation changes in the present time. Such emotional narratives can then become the basis of language. Language will rarely do justice to these rich and subtle nuances of experience except perhaps in poetry.

As psychotherapists we are still engaged in this kind of absorbing music with our clients as we attend to their stories and their way of relating them to us within the time and place that frame this specific kind of relating. Through the words and the spaces between the words, we feel our way into their world and meanings, and endeavour to show a willingness to explore and be open to them. Far more is involved than simply the narrative content itself. Instead it is as if we are living in a textural and ambient place or space with possibilities or restrictions of movement and feeling. In short, the lived experience of both our existences is palpable in some way through these subtle intimations of movement and feeling as a kind of atmosphere.

Are we always social beings?

How is it then that we feel we have access to the inner world of another? Colwyn Trevarthen[4] maintains that the infant's intersubjectivity is there within the womb. From his extensive research carried out with infants, he proposes that it is not surprising that communication is possible from birth.

> It is in the nature of human consciousness to experience being experienced: to be an actor who can act in relation to other conscious sources of agency, and to be a source of emotions while accepting emotional qualities of vitality and feeling from other persons by instant empathy. (p. 121)

Furthermore, this potential for rapport of the self with another mind appears to exist within the core of our consciousness as an 'unrational, unverbalised, conceptless, totally atheoretical, valency'. So research has shown how the infant appears to be aware of human presence and to follow this and engage with inner states of others. Trevarthen locates these tendencies within basic motives for relating with others. As such, inner states are accessible in behaviour and are signalled to them. Like Merleau-Ponty, he argues that perception in this sense is not separable from action. We create schemas or patterns for approaching others and environment and these are derived from a synthesis of sensory, motor and affective experiences. Greeting someone involves feeling, intention, specific movements in specific sequences, certain ways of attending to facial expressions and movements of others, and gauging appropriate and attuned responses. All these elements may be combined in one 'greeting and meeting' schema with variations for different contexts. These schemas of body, feeling and mind can then become coherent entities of experience about self, although they may arise from several different modalities of perception at the same time.

Trevarthen defines motive as 'a cause and director of movement, and, at the same time, a seeker of information to direct and confirm movement – to make it work for a purpose' (p. 123). However, another way of understanding such motives is as emotional states, and it is these which Trevarthen argues the other perceives as 'symptoms' of inner activity. In movement and gestures we communicate flows of affective states to each other and it is these which are resonant for the other. In the reverberations of flows and phrases of movement expressed through different communicative avenues – body, voice, facial expression, touch, etc. – baby and adult can become attuned or action patterns can become 'entrained'.

Origins of the sense of self with others

Daniel Stern[8] has argued that the infant begins life already with a nascent sense of self rooted in capacities for coherence, agency, continuity and affectivity. During the first eighteen months of life it develops increasingly modulated aspects of relating to others.

From the substantial body of research into infant social development, it appears that infants start in life primed for exploration and attention to particular aspects of the environment. A primary focus is the mother's face. Rochat and Striano[9] in a recent overview of infant studies challenge the notion that the newborn infant is in a state of autism. They quote a study which showed that newborn infants responded differently to tactile stimulation depending on whether it originated from self or other. They tended to root more frequently to a researcher stroking their cheek rather than to self-stimulation.

Differentiation between these two possibilities apparently exists from the beginning of life. Infants also appear to be able to respond proprioceptively to cues from others from birth[9] such as sticking out one's tongue. They tend to select facelike drawings rather than others. Whereas these and other behaviours appear to indicate a differentiation from and an attunement to others, Rochat and Striano argue that at this stage infants do not seem to be engaging in reciprocal relationships or any deliberate exploration of others. The stance is attentional rather than engaged, and this links with the limitations of movement that are possible at this stage.

Communication of feeling as basis for development

When there is a situation in which the mother is not responsive to the communicative readiness and signals of the infant, or does not approach with warmth and concern and inviting interest, the baby does not engage with her. This could also occur if the responses were appropriate but not offered at the right time. The baby may withdraw gaze or not smile, and this may also affect the mother's capacity to respond or to make 'conversation' with the baby.

Sandra Pipp[10] argues that the generation of emotions and

intersubjective perception appears to have a unique function in regulating learning and memory. It could be said then that how infants feel and how they pick up how others feel is central both to learning and creating a sense of self as memory. Emotional processes carry what she calls 'the cognitive prospectuses' of what is needed for communication. The self can only transfer meanings from others in a cooperative and mutual way and so this becomes a kind of template for transfer of meaning in relation to events and objects. In other words information that is not mediated by a personal way of relating to the infant has no intrinsic meaning and is not utilized by the infant. This would be like putting a baby in front of a television to learn something.

In observation of infant and carers Pipp reports that micro-levels of information exchange in affective states are communicated between infant and carer. These involve levels of excitement, exploration, attachment, attribution of meanings, qualities of movement and phrasing and rhythms. The mother plays a vital role in successfully attuning and affirming these dimensional embodied states of the infant. In her response the mother appears to help regulate and organize self-experiences. Experiences do not just come at the baby in a chaotic form; the mother is creating sequences and relationships between events and feelings which are communicated to the baby. So in this two-way process, the infant is able to incorporate this modality of the other within his or her own sense of coherence as these are repeated. Within the process is a lot of mismatching, negotiating, trial and error, all operating in a way to allow what Stern calls 'moving along'.[11,12] It involves a kind of 'fitting' with the infant, a mutual recognition of each other's motives and desires and feelings and this in turn signals a sense of sharing.

Again, these intricacies of learning and feeling in relationship that occur with carer and child can be helpful in our thinking about relationship processes in therapy. It is indicative of the need to consider the therapeutic relationship more dynamically as an embodied interactive system of perception, response, misalliance and meeting. But in order to be more aware of what is implicit, different attentional capacities have to be developed that capture some of these micro-moments of meeting.

Affect attunement

From the work of Stern,[8] Trevarthen,[4] Schore[7] and others, the primary constituent of infant–carer relationships is orchestrated in the capacity of the carer to attune to the child's expressive gestures and nonverbal communications. What is suggested by all this work is that this capacity is an intrinsic aspect of engagement. We do not think about what is happening, translate it into words or concepts and then act. We respond in varying degrees of synchrony with the movement rhythms and phrasings of the infant. We join in with something that is going on and make it up as we go along. This is shown in mirroring facial expressions, sounds, movements and so on. It is also more subtly shown in slight variations in all these spheres: slight modification, extension, prolonging or exaggerating or increasing or decreasing the intensity of movements and sounds. Both infant and carer respond to each other. Each appears to encourage or discourage continuation, the baby may appear to communicate more and for longer or may turn away and curl up if he or she wishes to desist. If the baby does not receive reciprocal communications with the carer, he or she will also tend to give up trying and over time will tend to mirror the carer's response instead. The baby appears to be more aroused and excited by the carer's joining in; some element is enhanced within its experiencing of itself with the other.

Affect attunement is conveyed by relative matching of phrasing, intensity, shape and flow of the baby. It can be expressed within the same sensory modalities or transposed to different ones. The capacity to attune affectively requires a sensitivity to focus on the other and for this focus to be felt by the other also. Attunement denotes an adjustment and a kind of fit to the resonances created by the movement field of the other. It requires a capacity to discern what is invariant among variant flux. In a visual sense, when we focus our vision, we narrow the field and exclude extraneous objects within that field.

Mismatching

Sometimes there may be a variety of resonances which create dissonance. The baby is both tired and wanting more stimuli at the same time. It is hungry and tired and so pushes food away. Or it could happen that the carer has their own preoccupations and is either depressed or excited and cannot sufficiently match the state of the infant. In fact, attunement is an ongoing process of continual good or bad fits. Within the overall relationship over time, Allen Schore[7] suggests that what is significant is the attempt to adjust and make fit which is important for the baby's learning of regulation of affective states or managing transitions. Transitions themselves are an indication of a different phase of attunement which needs to be adopted. Self-soothing capacities arise from this experience of modifying attunement. In the same way, therapists may find their interventions with clients as not being 'right', not hitting the right spot or not being close enough to the client's sense of things. This can strike a dissonant chord between therapist and client which has to be acknowledged and attended to before the relational process can continue.

Shifts of sensory modality in attunement

As Trevarthen has shown,[4] mothers and infants are motivated and respond to each other through emotional resonance. This can be expressed through imitation. However, Stern stresses that this is not enough since the infant must also recognize some correspondence to itself. Usually the initial communication and imitation occurs through the same sensory modality but the mother may introduce variations on the theme. At about nine months, another change appears to happen. At this stage, the mother may mirror correspondence through different sensory modalities. Examples of these could be a bodily movement that resonates in intensity and phrasing with the sound of the child, the mother could respond with a shape of sound to match the facial expression of the child, or she could rock her body to match the shaking movement of a rattle. It may also be more subtly embedded within an overall communication sequence. However, within the dimensions of intensity, timing and shape, matching forms can resonate with intensity, contour, beat, rhythm duration and shape.

Attunement to inner state and influence on feeling

What is significant about this is that imitation within the sensory modality focuses attention on the external form of behaviour. Affect attunement recasts the expression so that it is referring more directly to the inner experience behind the original form and it signals a kind of recognition or resonance with an inner state through movement. It appears that affect attunement can indicate a primary capacity of connection of ourselves with others prior to conceptual elaboration or language. However, these affect attunements also contribute the basis for the development of language. Schore's work[7] emphasizes the regulatory effect that the mother has on the baby in their mutual communicating. As has been noted such affective regulation helps the baby manage transitions from one state which is important in self-soothing. For example, how do we cope when we are feeling very distressed? How do we help ourselves feel better or comfort ourselves? Some kind of supportive inner dialogue or process is needed when we hit critical moments. It could be argued that much of psychotherapy contributes to this kind of allowing inner space for different states of feeling rather than exorcising them.

Attunement and narcissistic injury

Allen Schore has investigated the biological effects of the mother–child relationship in the development of the brain and nervous system.[7] Schore relates the processes of affect attunement or lack to narcissistic damage. He describes this in terms of shame. Schore speculates that when infants do not find attunement from others they experience a sense of self misattuned with a 'self-dysregulating' other. This is an early proto-experience of shame, and can lead both to a disposition to further experiences which echo these and to more difficulties in managing or regulating the feelings that arise. Whereas it can be surmised that the infant's sense of self with an attuned, smiling and engaged other creates a positive sense of self with other, when this is not found the infant is likely to have imprinted a core sense of self misattuned to by a non-responsive other. The sense of self is thus equated with the opposite of esteem which could be shame. This has powerful effects on maturation according to Schore. He relates the research from infant/carer patterns to the manifestation of difficulties in psychotherapeutic patients. In patients suffering from narcissistic problems, the patient's socioaffective transactions are guided by an internalized working model of interactive misattunement, and these representations encode expectations of humiliating narcissistic assault from a primary object.

If the caregiver can mediate affective states within herself and her infant, then the infant is likely to be able to manage shifts of state more successfully – for example, from grandiosity to shyness. Without affect attunement, emotions remain difficult to access or experience.

Schore therefore argues for the psychotherapist utilizing ways of attuning to the patient nonverbally as a way to facilitate psychotherapeutic change. This requires the therapist, consciously and, importantly, unconsciously, to:

affectively resonate with the patient, allowing him or herself to stay emotionally connected with, and available to the patient during the oscillating separation and reunion periods of the dynamic transference that occur over the course of the therapeutic relationship ...

The recognition and acceptance of the patient's shame lies at the heart of empathic listening in the analytic process. (p. 459)[7]

Schore locates both narcissistic and borderline problems developmentally to specific differences within brain development occurring in the right frontal limbic area of the brain and right hemisphere which regulates emotions and relational capacities. Since these refer to the disorganization of primitive affects, again, he emphasizes that what will be needed from the therapist will be attunement and sensitivity to the nonverbal aspects of affect communication. With the strong focus on the mother's face in early infancy, Schore suggests that the stress on facial exposure and on visual aspects of the felt experience of shame may reflect the central imprinting effect of the mother's face within the schemas that are created. Voice and tone of voice may also be powerful in earlier affective reactions. The goal is to facilitate homeostatic self-regulatory systems of affect that would normally evolve during the relational process of mother–infant interactions.

Within the work of psychotherapy, therapists are frequently confronted with clients who have experienced many difficulties in receiving attuned attention. This may be manifested in a variety of ways. It may be difficulty in attending to their own experiencing in any sustained way without feeling impinged or intruded on by others so that there is a sense of blankness or having nothing to say. It may be expressed in angry feelings towards the therapist who always fails to make the right kind of intervention or response. It may be masked by a sustained self-doubt or attack on any inner affective impulses, experienced as a sense of shame and unworthiness.

Preverbal sense of self

In sum, the proposal is made that there is a sense of self before we even begin to speak. Whereas psychologists have tended to emphasize the need for a capacity for representation and symbolization to facilitate the emergence of 'I', studies on infants appear to suggest that a sense of self can be discerned from birth. Such a self is manifested in an orientation towards rapport or communication with others.[4] According to Stern[8] it is also manifested in capacities for coherence, organizing experiences such as shown by babies' preference for variations on a theme in games. Babies also show capacities to make choices, have feelings and to have a sense of a continuing existence in their recognition of patterns of events. These aspects of self and self in relation to others appear to go through three crucial shifts during the first year of life. Daniel Stern[8] designates three stages in terms of an emergent self from birth to 2 months when the infant is beginning to form relations between isolated moments of experience and processes that occur. There is a core self from 2 to 6 months, when the infant begins to gather moments of organized coherence into invariant patterns or schemas. The unfolding of a subjective self from 7 months to the development of language around 15 months develops as the infant recognizes that both self and others have minds, and that the 'subject matter' of the mind is potentially shareable (p. 124). At 15 months another shift of self occurs with language and a verbal sense of self.

But crucially, for Stern, these senses of self, once formed, continue to coexist throughout human life in parallel forms. They do not disappear and they do not lose their value and meaning. As adults we continue to live from many different senses of self. For example, the emergent self has to do with what is emerging in awareness, as yet unnamed but felt. This resembles the experience of first impressions of a new country where nothing is familiar. We also live from a sense of core embodiment in which there are varying degrees of boundedness, containment and coherence. At different times in our life we feel connected or less connected with our bodies. Areas of bodily/affective experience that have not been acknowledged or symbolized in words can be symbolized bodily as somatic symptoms.

As has been stressed throughout this chapter, we are able to meet each other nonverbally through our intersubjective selves which are attuned to picking up subtle micro-cues from small changes in movement and expression. We are living in this domain all the time.

Finally, we are accustomed to considering ourselves as verbal selves conducting life through words (but sometimes forgetting or ignoring what underpins the possibilities of language). Psychotherapy is a domain of relating which needs to encompass all these aspects of self. These may be addressed implicitly or explicitly. Words enable experiences to be acknowledged in a very direct and specific communication; other ways of experiencing remain more ambiguous and multi-dimensional but no less tangible and real.

Stern[8] identified many fascinating and useful facets to these notions of preverbal senses of self. The most relevant of these concerns the sharing of affective states. He reported on the experiments where infants are exposed to an apparent visual cliff while drawn towards a highly attractive and different kind of toy. Their ambivalence is controlled by the infants' evident seeking of the mother's facial expression which will inform them of how they should feel and react. In other words, it is only because infants can have a sense of the mother possessing particular affects that enables them to seek information in this way. As adults, we still tend to check the emotional responses of others quite closely, especially if we are telling a joke or disclosing something potentially shocking.

An example of how facial expressions become interwoven with self once occurred in my own therapeutic practice. A client expressed a lot of rage towards me. Later she said she had watched my face very closely to see how I reacted. When it appeared I was open to her anger, she had felt a profound shift. She related how she had walked down the road still with this image of my face while she was angry. She felt freed. It seemed to be a moment where she gained an entirely different perspective on herself, seeing herself walk down the street with this consciousness of my reaction to this experience. It could be surmised that the gaze of another in receipt of her communication opened a new experience of herself with others that was freeing in some way. What may be added here is that she had also informed me before that she could never remember people's faces at all.

Describing the implicit

The work of Stern[8,11,12] and others mentioned in this chapter has excited many people because it has dared to name and explicate some of these pre-attentional processes in relationships – especially in the context of infant development. Latterly, Stern[12] has reshaped earlier terms into one overarching concept which he designates '*vitality contours*'.

> There are internal subjective events consisting ... of the continual, instant-by-instant shifts in feeling state, resulting in an array of temporal feeling flow patterns that we will call vitality contours. (p. 67)

For infants, there is a beginning, a middle and end to multiple vitality contours which may be formed around a repetitive activity of putting to bed, or to a new kind of game between adult and infant. A vitality contour would then provide a moment of self-experiencing in terms of a kind of emotional narrative for this moment.

Several examples may be given of how we notice vitality contours in our work with clients. Consider how each of our clients arrives, enters and leaves the room for therapy. Each will have evolved certain patternings of movement and feeling and action that have recognizable shapes. One may come in and be still and silent for a long time. Another will have certain ways of arranging their coat. Another will arrive and start speaking before they have sat down. Throughout each session, there will be different sequences of flow and movement synchronized through narrative, voice tone, body movements, expressions. It is not the content of these events that is being described here; it is the way that moments are travelled through to arrive at the next point. It is the how. Sometimes these patternings can be described as transferences. Sometimes they are recognizable within parallel processes which occur in supervision when it is as if the group or supervision process becomes caught into a similar rhythm and phrasing of experiencing. This would be a vitality contour.

Dance is based on these shapings of feeling. A recent work from Denmark used Tchaikovsky's *Sleeping Beauty* score to counterpose a modern version of the story. The daughter's dysfunctional family life is blighted by drug addiction rather than the wicked fairy who has been excluded from the christening. The choreographer utilized a repetitive motif in all the sequences of movement. It began as an expansive and more sustained arc of movement outward which seemed positive and joyful, then it would abruptly turn inwards with bound flow. In this way, a vitality contour showed a pattern of interrupted feeling and flow, cutting off something. An urge to go towards or to go outwards suddenly turns back against itself. This repetitive movement sequence gives the ballet an edgy, disturbing quality, in fact, like drug addiction.

Music and the flow of relating

If we attempt to get closer to the vague sphere of experiencing and responding within therapy, a useful analogy could be our response to music. Langer[13] describes how music is meaningful to us because it echoes our felt experience. She describes how music may convey a rich kaleidoscope of shifting meaning as we listen.

> The imagination that responds to music is personal and associative and logical, tinged with affect, tinged with bodily rhythm, tinged with dream, but concerned with a wealth of formulations for its wealth of wordless knowledge, its whole knowledge ... the ways of living and dying and feeling. Because no assignment of meaning is conventional, none is permanent beyond the sound that passes; yet the brief association was a flash of understanding. (p. 244)

She goes on to stress how meaning is not assigned in some pre-existing way. It comes and passes with each sound. The effect that lasts and is important is the way something has been made 'conceivable' in the same way that speech originally makes something conceivable. It is not that we 'store up propositions'. The gift of music is not communication but insight; in a very naïve phrase, it is a knowledge of 'how feelings go'.

Music sounds like the way moods feel. In the interpersonal flow of therapist and client, there is the same attempt to allow something to be formed that fits how the moods feel in this endeavour to understand and to make sense of. A lasting impression is the summation of these micro-moments of relationship which lingers as a distinct after-taste, or the felt sense of the person and situation. It is a process which affects both people. Both have inhabited a shared experiencing time and space together like music.

Merleau-Ponty[6] talks about self and other weaving a common fabric from sharing language together. 'Understanding' is not an intellectual abstraction removed from experience.

> To understand is to experience the harmony between what we aim at and what is given, between the intention and the performance, – and the body is our anchorage in the world ...We say that the body has understood and habit has been cultivated when it has absorbed a new meaning, and assimilated a fresh core of significance. (pp. 146–147)

Example

One clinical example comes to mind to illustrate these ideas more concretely. This involved a client who had learned to live within a precarious domain in herself, feeling very exposed as if stranded on the surface of her skin, without an inside bodily safe place; at the same time she felt very cut off from others. At one and the same time she suffered feelings of shame and exposure and also isolation. It meant initially that the style of communication was distanced and rather cynical, and on an intellectual and arid level.

In one session she relayed a time in her life when she had gone for a walk on her own after a traumatic experience. As I listened to her, I felt as if I could feel this walk somatically with her, the sense of the specific environment, the wind blowing and the kind of aloneness that contained her and also emphasized her sense of isolation. At one point, the wind was so strong that she could lean back on it. The felt sense of two distinct qualities appeared – one of a huddled figure battling against fate, the other a kind of letting go and leaning into support. These kinaesthetic characteristics touched directly into an experiencing of a kind of polarity within her – between isolating and managing by herself and letting go to a sense of environmental support. She could draw on these in a new, more embodied way to discover new possibilities. They were a kind of deconstructed metaphor – mobilized in a multimodal blend of movement, sensory experience, feeling and emotional state. By accessing some of these aspects very directly within myself as I listened to her, and sharing this, there seemed to be a way of touching closely something that did not as yet have words or names. There was something that seemed to get closer to the sense of the possibility of being alone in the company of another, of a kind of reverie containing and gathering experience into new meanings between us. This is an example of affect attunement. It required a resonating with a bodily experiencing and a recasting of this in reflection back to match something known but not symbolized before.

These and similar moments in our work seemed to contribute to a distinct shift in the quality of her contact and relations with the world, as the sense of shame and exposure gradually disappeared. She said that she had found a place inside herself where she felt safe and protected. When she left, she had the aim of letting herself lie on the grass in the summer and enjoying the present in an entirely new way, because before she did not live in the present at all but was always vigilant to manage the next threat of exposure. Perhaps, then, this notion of attuning to the inner sense of things was a helpful response in confirming an inner sense of self as a nonverbal source of being and feeling.

What is valued by clients?

Research with clients also points to what is experienced as helpful in psychotherapy. In a recent study concerned with what clients valued from their therapists, each client identified various aspects of what it meant to be heard.[14] The aspects reported reflect in a highly resonant way the ideas that have emerged about how mothers interact with their infants. It was also clear that nonverbal aspects were very important in clients' perception of a counsellor's attention:

> Eye contact, she would look at me, she'd be there with me... yes you know her eyes never wandered and her mind was on what she had to do. I really felt that she listened to what I had to say. [This made me feel] that somebody cared.

There was also an appreciation of words given back in a different way that could lead the client into different words and feelings. The therapist's capacity to synthesize her experience and to provide a perspective was useful, as was her capacity to allow for and understand the feeling of self-hate within the person's experience. Also the feeling of somehow being refuelled by the attention and care: 'I felt as though I was moving in leaps and bounds, that I felt really good about myself. I thought, "I'm really progressing here"!'

Within some exchanges there has been an element of shared feeling of jokes that emphasizes a kind of mutuality and intersubjectivity, such as the mother amplifying a response from the infant. There was a security in the relationship: 'I felt secure in moving with him. I never felt that he'd take me further than I could handle.'

There was also a sense that the therapist could bear difficult feelings or realize how truly awful a person's experience had been without flinching from it. In this sense, we can see how Schore's concept of affect regulation makes sense in this context.

It seems also that a quality of something unfolding as the relationship goes on creates a more background ambience of empathy or attunement rather than specific moments *per se*. This becomes a kind of ground in which the relationship is construed. The specificity of attention was also a vital part of the process; it was personal and concrete, and therefore provided a feeling of the therapist being really in touch with the client.

Stern's work on change in psychotherapy[11]

Why is all this important for psychotherapists? The research on development through relational contact between babies and carers suggests that these aspects of relationship may continue to be important throughout life. Within the therapeutic relationship, both parties are responding primarily through feeling and experiencing to the cues and responses of each other in order to continue and move along, whatever emerges from the interaction.

A recent paper by Stern and his associates[11] places the significance of the implicit relational knowing in the foreground of therapeutic change. Rather than a vague background accompaniment to dialogue, Stern proposes that this implicit intersubjective attunement and response leads to significant moments of change, designated *now* moments when something different happens that is mutually shared as a specifically heightened, affective and intense moment. The new moment jolts both parties to go beyond usual patternings and to discover some new relational bond. These moments are those cited by clients as indicating key moments of change. They correspond to the 'something more than' understandings that may also have been reached and valued within therapeutic change.

Summary and application for therapy

I would propose several important themes arise for psychotherapists in the understanding of intersubjectivity that emerges from the field of observation of infant development and early social cognition. These themes point us towards more essential aspects of relationship and towards understanding how therapeutic relational processes are to us.

There is intrinsic intersubjectivity that leads us to be sensitive and highly attuned to each other's inner states manifested in many nonverbal dimensions. It may be argued from a developmental viewpoint or from an experiential perspective that a core aspect of therapeutic work is conveying a sense of sharing of this nonverbal self experiencing and that this is also facilitated by finding a shared language to communicate this. There are some very important moments of meaning where a sense of sharing and connection is particularly important for clients. This involves attunement, engaging and finding meaning emergent in the process. These in turn reflect patterns of vitality contours, patterns of relationship and senses of self with other that continue to grow in complexity and meaning or depth. Certain emotional difficulties are especially rooted in these earlier senses of self with others and may not respond well to overly conceptual interventions or ones that repeat early shame/misattuned experiences. Attunement can be more important than intellectual constructs.

Primary senses of self are a co-creation of self with other through sharing feeling states and are therefore experienced as bodily feeling senses of self. This means that the therapeutic process provides an opportunity for a new sense of self with other to come into being. Both are mutually engaged, and bodily experiencing is a vital tool in attuning to and communicating this understanding either verbally or nonverbally.

Affect attunement is a core way for individuals to feel understood from inside. It is demonstrated not only by mirroring but by recasting what is being expressed in other sensory modalities which capture the vitality contours of what has been said. When this is achieved, the person feels that the inner feeling of what has been expressed in a specific form but reflected in a different way has been heard. Attunement is akin to focusing vision where extraneous information is screened out to narrow and deepen attention to one aspect. It is perceived as a sense of being touched or being in direct contact with the other's attention. When there is misattunement this can be experienced as not being met or in contact and may re-evoke painful past experiences.

Conclusion

This chapter has looked at how feeling informs our way of engaging with others. The existence of a nonverbal sense of self and an implicit grasping of others' feelings and inner states is something that we have lived with all our lives. As therapists, we use these parts of our consciousness more explicitly. The argument put forward by Schore, Stern and others is that more primary aspects of relating such as affect attunement play a vital part in connecting with the deeper senses of self and in symbolizing new meanings in a shared human context.

In the next chapter, further exploration is undertaken to

consider three basic questions: How do we know what is going on? How is feeling related to our sense of knowing? How does this have any bearing on our work as psychotherapists?

2 | Knowing and Feeling – How Do We Know What We Know?

> We do not know anything about our own bodies, we cannot know. At best we can take a dead body, and cut it in pieces, and there are some who can take a live animal and cut it in pieces in order to see what is inside the body. Still, that has nothing to do with our own bodies. We know very little about them. Why do we not? Because our attention is not discriminating enough to catch very fine movements that are going on within. We can know of them only when the mind becomes more subtle and enters, as it were, deeper into the body. To get the subtle perceptions we have to begin with the grosser perceptions. We have to get hold of that which is setting the whole engine in motion.[1]

Sound, which, as a deeper ear, hears us, who appear to be hearing[2]

So far, my task has been to propose that feeling or heart is the base of knowing and relationship. It is a kind of implicit knowing and it allows us to connect with others in multidimensional and profound ways. It begins in infancy and continues throughout life. As therapists we begin to become more conscious of the micro processes of awareness and contact that are going on in our meetings with clients. Stern *et al.* have suggested that this base of implicit relating contributes to fundamental shifts where client and therapist find a new sense of meeting each other in novel or unfamiliar ways.[3] It facilitates a different sense of self with other. It is that sudden awareness of feeling newly present with another person. It can be noticing the glance of another at the same time as you glance at them. It can be a funny moment of knowing that you know that he knows! It is an experience where we feel as if we discover what relationship means for the first time *again.*

In this chapter, I want to go further with considering how feeling and thought and language go together. When we separate body from mind, or experience from thought, or feeling from words, we conjure up a sense of separate worlds like planets. If words and thoughts are from Mars, then feelings and experience are from Venus! Feelings and experience are highly suspect, unreliable and frustratingly amorphous. Words and thoughts specify, delineate and firmly locate things in a specific place. They are reliable. Experience is so unnameable it defies thinking about. Yet we navigate the world by it.

Among the many diverse views on these issues, I would like to include principally three perspectives that shed interesting light on how these apparently different worlds may, in fact, come from the same planet. I will name this planet Earth and this Earth is the ground of sentience and feeling. The perspectives I include are mainly from Francisco Varela, Evan Thompson and Eleanor Rosch, whose work integrates perspectives drawn from phenomenology, neuroscience, cognitive psychology and Buddhist philosophy.[4] The second perspective comes from James Gibson who proposed an ecological approach to perception.[5] The third comes from Antonio Damasio who has offered a model of consciousness which integrates the felt sense of experiencing with neuroscience.[6]

What we have seen in the previous chapter is that perception of self and other is bidirectional. In her response to the child, the mother appears to help regulate and organize self-experiences. In this two-way process, the infant is able to take on the mother's responses within his or her own sense of coherence as these are repeated. Within the process is a lot of mismatching, negotiating, trial and error, all operating in a way that allows what Stern calls 'moving along'.[7] It involves a kind of 'fitting' with the infant, a mutual recognition of each other's motives and desires and feelings, and this in turn signals a sense of sharing. This way of understanding the infant dyad as a system suggests the need to consider the therapeutic relationship more dynamically as an embodied system involving perception, response, misalliance and meeting.

As therapists, this is territory through which we boldly stride in every session without too much thought. We feel we can find ways of accessing experiencing within another and to explicate this in our responses and engagement with our clients. We do not usually bother to think too much about how we can do this.

Gendlin's felt sense

Eugene Gendlin has been concerned for many years with the relationship between experiencing and the creation of meaning.[8,9] This has led to valuable formulations of experiencing prior to language in his concept of the 'felt sense'. In his work on the experiential process in psychotherapy, Gendlin has tried to formulate the essential aspects of therapeutic movement. This requires an accessing of experience as a somatically felt vague sense, a gathered constellation of feeling, thinking, experiencing which can be allowed to come into foreground awareness as a touchstone for discerning meaning. It requires a capacity to tolerate vague edges, unclear senses and the fuzzy side of experiences until meaning becomes clear. As we shall see, this notion fits well with the theories of neuroscientist Antonio Damasio, who describes a parallel vision to this in neurobiological language when he discusses the process of brain activity as a number of different systems of perception operating at roughly the same time.[10] There is no one place where all these networks of information coincide, but some organizing process operates to provide us with the sense of a unified experience. In *Focusing*, Gendlin emphasizes the value of allowing time for all the vague aspects of an experience to come into awareness, so that a new way of symbolizing or carrying forward new meaning can happen.[8] It takes patience and a capacity to stay open without knowing.

Top–down versus bottom–up processing

This account of a therapeutic process can be compared to a related concept. Cognitive psychologists have formulated models of perception which clarify these two processes of experience and meaning further.[11] One is the *top–down* model. We use existing schemes of cognition and perception to organize and understand a new experience – such as getting a ticket at a station in a new country. We have patterns of experience which we can apply to help us. Therapists may approach clients with theories that are also intended to help organize the understanding of material so that it makes sense within a theoretical model. The opposite way of perceiving is to create patterns from raw experience, called the *bottom–up* approach. This would be akin to how we respond when we hear entirely new forms of music, or meet a person from a very different culture, or how we learn to use a computer or foreign language from scratch. In therapy, the bottom–up approach would be akin to a person-centred, or phenomenological approach. No pattern is assumed. Each person and situation needs specific attention that is minimally distorted by previous sedimented expectations. As therapists, we probably move between both of these perspectives of bottom–up and top–down processing all the time.

Biological processes and experience

So what do we mean by experiencing?

At a simple biological level we know that we are informed interoceptively and proprioceptively. These are terms which simply describe how we perceive stimuli arising from the body especially from the movement and position of the body, and through our current felt experience. We are constantly affected by something else happening all the time. From a very simple biological point of view, the nervous system is utilizing shifting sets of neural connections and systems, stimulated by innumerable chemical messengers throughout the body. We notice twinges and tensions and relaxations, we notice feeling down or up or expansive or shut down and so on. We may or may not be aware of these seething inner landscapes which involve every surface and form and process going on. Apart from physical sensory experiencing, we may also notice a subliminal flow of imagery-like dreams. With such vast informational processes, the subtleties of simultaneous moment-by-moment experience within the therapist and client are beyond the scope of this kind of representation. We can feel all these layers at once, but it is infinitely harder to break them all down into pieces and name them. Yet it is the qualities of feeling within these processes which appear to be most significant in clients' experience of the therapy and in change.

The central problem for theorists in this area is how experience becomes the stuff of feeling and thinking and images. Franciso Varela is a cognitive psychologist who originated from Chile. His original work with Humberto Maturana provided an integrated, evolutionary view of perception grounded in biological systems.[12] This model proposes a close interactive interface between biological systems and the environment so that one directly expresses the other. More recently Varela, Thompson and Rosch suggested that both Freud and earlier cognitive psychologists have made things complicated by separating experience from how it might be symbolized mentally before we can know about it.[4] Instead of a direct process of experience within the nervous system, these other models require that a middle agency has to be found to translate experience into a symbolic form.

However, Varela *et al.* propose an alternative and intuitively sensed fact that cognition and consciousness go together. What we know and how we know what we know are one process.

The idea of self-organizing systems

The first principle to grasp here is that the systems of perception and cognition continue to become more complex during development. Donald Hebb proposed in 1949 that learning could be based on changes in the brain which resulted from the degree that neurons correlated or worked together.[13] If two neurons tend to be active together their connection is strengthened; otherwise it is weakened. These connections created transformations related to patterns of neural networks involved in specific tasks. Over time, a kind of automatizing occurs whereby subsystems of cells work together. This is a model of emergent self-organizing systems that is continuously being brought into new configurations. Another way of considering such subsystems and patterns is that they represent schemas in which intention, movement, affect, perception are all simultaneous.

How perception guides action

If we are claiming that perception involves learned schemas of orientation and behaviour, then it is clearer that perception is not a passive process in which we simply receive information like a blank sheet of paper. Varela *et al.* coin the word 'enaction' to describe the interplay of both subject and environment.[4] They argue that perception here consists of 'perceptually guided action' and 'cognitive structures' that emerge from the recurrent sensorimotor patterns that enable action to be perceptually guided (p. 173). Cognition is embodied action. A chicken approach would suppose that the world out there possessed existing pre-given properties which our system has to recover. The egg position would be that the cognitive system projects its own world. 'The apparent reality of the world is merely a reflection of internal laws of the system.'

Varela *et al.* argue for a third position where both are engaged through embodied action. There is no additional representation process. What they mean by *embodied* is that cognition is dependent on having a body with various sensorimotor capacities and that these themselves are embedded in a more encompassing biological, psychological and cultural context. Supporting this approach is an extensive discussion of the perception of colour which illustrates how colour is neither existing as a pre-given nor is something that is entirely our own construal. In the stress on action, they reiterate how cognition is not separable from sensorimotor processes, perception and action.

Contrary to a representative approach where what is out in the world has to be decoded through some kind of symbolization within our brains, their view of perception is one which starts with how the perceiver can guide his actions in a local situation. Since these continually change with the perceiver's activity it is more a question of how the perceiver is embodied/situated/orientated which discloses different perceptions. This insight is one that the French phenomenologist and psychologist Merleau-Ponty anticipated:

> The organism cannot properly be compared to a keyboard on which the external stimuli would play and in which their proper form would be delineated for the simple reason that the organism contributes to the constitution of that form.... The properties of the object and the intentions of the subject ... are not only intermingled; they also constitute a new whole. (p. 13)[14]

Bodily based meaning, imagination and reason

Mark Johnson has also shown how meaning, imagination and reason have a bodily basis in the mind.[15] Since basic structures in thought and language derive from early bodily sensorimotor schemas they become embedded within the evolving networks that Hebb described.[13] For example, Johnson shows that concepts such as inside–outside and containment, or the experience of force on a system, or the experience of walking all have links to adult logical thought processes. Concepts of containers – what belongs in one place and not in another – would be intrinsic to mathematical concepts of sets and subsets and theories of logic. The experience of force on a system becomes imbued in metaphors about 'countering' or 'opposing arguments'. Even the flow of logic is linked with an emergent bodily schema of walking continuously along (source–path–goal schema). Metaphors are directly reflecting schemas or organizations of movement, image and preverbal qualities of experiencing.

Physiognomic perception

Werner and Kaplan who were Gestalt psychologists in the 1960s were interested in how physiognomic aspects of experiencing continue to be accessible in language.[16] They carried out a large number of experiments where they asked participants to draw shapes that corresponded with words. They also showed different groups lines and shapes and asked them to indicate the feeling/meaning of these shapes. There were some very interesting correspondences. From both perspectives, it was clear that words continue to have physiognomic and experiential qualities although we may not be conscious of this until we start reflecting on it. For example, the word *soft* sounds like it feels; also *hard, wool, wood or break*. It is not only the onomatopoeic qualities that are encoded, but we also imbue words with our physiognomic associations. Werner and Kaplan maintained that when we hear words we apply the earlier sensorimotor and affective schemas that conjure up its meaning. Suppose we come across a tree trunk in a wood. If we decided to use it as a table we would conjure up very different physiognomic associations of table-based experience as opposed to if we called it a chair – where sitting experiences would be evoked. As therapists, we learn to pay attention to the way clients use words and the kinds of more subliminal experiential qualities that are evoked below their surface content. This is particularly clear if clients repeat specific words or phrases; for example, supposing a client kept saying that they had 'just had enough of it', or another client who says they 'do not know', within both phrases lie deeper bases of experiences and cognitions that need to be unpacked in their embodied sense.

James Gibson's model of perception

So far, in summary, the model of perception that is emerging is one which involves a holistic and dynamic understanding. Words and conceptions are imbued with more primary experiential qualities. James Gibson was a cognitive psychologist in the 1970s.[5] His approach to perception marked a radical move from more orthodox approaches. He maintained that perceptual systems have evolved to assist an organism's navigation or orientation in an environment. It is not a static environment. He questioned the whole basis of research which had led to the understanding of perception. He was concerned that models of perception had been derived from static laboratory experiments, usually stressing visual perception.

Gibson argues that in evolutionary terms, organisms and humans needed to move fast through changing terrains. Perceptual systems are adapted in relation to environmental systems. One cannot be separated from the other. They co-define themselves. Gibson proposed that the primary way perception occurs is through the pick-up of environmental cues. These are provided by the ambient array emitted by laminations of surface textures. We can understand this in a literal way by imagining how we adapt to negotiating woods, open spaces, crowded pavements or shopping centres. We are subliminally aware of gaps and densities, sequences of textural flows, and interruptions and changes in them.

Metaphorically, we may be aware of ourselves traversing life, relationships, books and films in the same way – experiencing myriad changing textural surfaces in the information they give us and the ambience and atmosphere that is provided from moment to moment. Evidently we select only a minimal number of conscious cues and reactions from these. Gibson stressed that *we do not live in space, we live in places*. In other words, space is not an abstract concept, it is known through our embodied inhabitation. Perception is thus a meeting place of adaptation between person and environment in which the environment is perceived as offering differing affordances or possibilities for the survival of the organism.

Gibson's theory of perception is of perceptual systems as achievements of the human organism, not an appearance of the theatre of his consciousness. It involves awareness *of* not just awareness. Sensory modalities are perceptual systems and perception is a psychosomatic act of a living observer. The act of picking up information is a ceaseless and unbroken activity. The sea of energy in which we live flows and changes without sharp breaks. Even the tiny fraction of this energy that affects the receptors is a flux, not a sequence. The continuous act of perceiving involves the co-perceiving of the self. Objects possess a variety of *affordances* from the surfaces they offer. For Gibson all the notions of imagining, dreaming, rationalizing and wishful thinking, remembering, judging and so on may be reconstrued within his conception of ecological perception.

> To perceive is to be aware of the surfaces of the environment and of oneself in it. The interchange between hidden and unhidden surfaces is essential to this awareness. These are existing surfaces; they are specified at some points of observation. Perceiving gets wider and finer and longer and richer and fuller as the observer explores the environment processes in each case.(p. 255)[5]

This point is important; Gibson reminds us that perception is an activity that continues to develop throughout life. Within specific different occupations, we develop further capacities to perceive – for example, health carers are skilled in detecting states of health from skin colour. Electrical engineers can detect fine levels of current. Gardeners notice plant conditions. Therapists learn to notice small but significant moments of shift and feeling during the therapeutic process.

Perception is about outside and inside at the same time
Another important aspect of this model is the reminder that all perceptual systems are proprioceptive as well as exteroceptive because they provide information about the perceiver's activities. This is often forgotten or unacknowledged within our cultural constructions of experience as being somehow *out there*. Information about the self is multiple including sensations on skin, muscles, sights, sounds and so on. From this perspective, the supposedly separate realms of subjective and objective are actually only 'poles of attention' according to Gibson.

> The information for 'in here' is of the same kind as the information for the perception of 'out there'. (p. 116)[5]

Our five perceptual systems correspond to five modes of overt and overlapping attention which are subordinated to an overall orienting system. Systems can orient, explore, investigate and adjust and so on. Perceptual systems can mature and learn. Sensations from one system can be associated with another; no new sensations are learned but the information that is picked up becomes more and more subtle, elaborate and precise with practice. So it is a lifelong process.

Varela *et al.* versus Gibson
Although this model of perception is also one that is direct and does not include representation, it is different from Varela *et al.*'s model.[4] This is because Gibson's approach is more orientated to the environmental cues than the perceiver's guided action. Perception is largely optical and centred more on the ways that the environment conveys information through invariances in

optical arrays. However, I would argue that the textural and surface elements within this model of perception require kinaesthetic or proprioceptively linked systems and the optical emphasis may be deceptive. The notion of the environment as offering affordances, and shifting opportunities based on spatial perception, is an interesting one to apply, at least as a metaphor to the role of the therapist. The therapist could be considered as environment or as transformational object, as Bollas suggests.[17]

The feeling of what happens: Antonio Damasio

Many of the ideas elaborated from different contributors and from different methodologies and philosophical assumptions also appear to correspond to some degree with the recent ground-breaking work of Antonio Damasio, a neuroscientist who bases much of his research and thinking on his work and experience with neurological patients.[6] He also points out how neuroscientific understanding has been enormously facilitated in the past decade by breakthroughs in the technical tools now available in research.

Damasio identifies the two central problems in theories and research on consciousness. The first is how we come to get a flow of moving images – like a film in our minds. The second is how we come to have an ongoing sense of self as we perceive these images; he conveys this expressively:

> There is a presence of you in a particular relationship with some object.... The presence is quiet and subtle, and sometimes it is little more than a 'hint half guessed', 'a gift half understood' to borrow words from T. S. Eliot. (p. 10)

Damasio proceeds by clarifying different aspects of consciousness. He initially offers the simplest definition from dictionaries 'that consciousness is the organism's awareness of its own self and its surroundings' (p. 4). Yet consciousness is not monolithic. It can be simple and complex. Whereas many contemporary models of consciousness have been focused on the complex levels of consciousness more clearly comparable with artificial intelligence and computer processing, Damasio intends to construct a model of consciousness from bottom–up rather than top–down approach. In such a model, the simpler level should be one that can be linked with the more complex levels, and his argument also includes a recognition of evolutionary systems.

Damasio gives fascinating and compassionate clinical examples to show how patients with neurological damage can be awake and not conscious, or able to use low-level attention to the environment without consciousness. Consciousness is not the same as wakefulness, nor the same as attention. In the manifestation of consciousness, normal organisms demonstrate wakefulness, attentiveness to surroundings and also context-appropriate behaviour which would include background emotions.

How do we perceive according to Damasio?

General understanding has for some time recognized that pure perception of an object within one sensory modality does not exist. The organism requires not only sensory signals but also signals from the adjustment of the body before perception may occur. Such a perception will result from how the sensory cortices form neural patterns – like maps across many different areas of the visual cortex working together. However, the same brain region would construct entirely different maps according to the different motor behaviour while the visual system changed. The parts of the brain which are mapping the body in order to make sure that the system is stable are constantly providing maps of body states. Again this reiterates the idea that different body positions would change the maps made of what is happening.

From these observations Damasio suggests that there are

two kinds of consciousness – one would be core and the other elaborated or autobiographical. These also correspond with two senses of self. A core sense of self is ceaselessly created anew with every moment of experiencing from this ongoing mapping, whereas the autobiographical self requires memory and systematized memories, and this involves more elaborate reiteration of existing mappings already held within many different areas which operate as dispositions or implicit procedures based on invariant experiences and specific events.

How do we get a sense of self?
Damasio suggests that two parallel mappings of body states are going on.[6] One is mapping what is going on and the other is mapping how this new mapping affects the current state of our organism. So as I sit here at my computer, my brain is mapping the physical location of my body, the activity in my fingers, the words I am thinking about and typing through the keyboard, sensations of my coffee as I drink it, emotions as I am doing all of this in the context of the time of day, the season, the weather and the ground in which all of this happens. These reflections require conscious effort and thought to know.

However, at the same time there is a more subtle presenced feeling going on to accompany all of this; it is not just fingers typing and a body sitting here, it is a sense of visceral closeness and intimacy to all of this which I feel as my self. This results from the secondary mapping process, how this background sense is subtly modified by each new moment. This is just simply known by me as a bodily felt sensing; it does not require more thought but only an attention and openness.

It is this to which we can have direct access. It is also important to stress here that background feeling is *the way the brain minds the body, it is the mapping process itself*. Therefore, it is a direct cognition. It would include a mental flow of images which are continuously unfolding and are not limited to visual representations. Images involve a synthesis of sensory modalities, sensory and affective elements. Damasio proposes that consciousness originates when this kind of wordless knowledge representing what is perceived is experienced also as creating a change within the organism. While we perceive something, we also perceive how in the perceiving we are affected by it. Such perception arises from the additional sensorimotor and affective responses. In other words, our sense of self arises from a parallel background feeling accompanying the object of our perception. Wordless knowledge arises in its simplest form at a mental level as a 'feeling of knowing'. Therefore, the original basis of consciousness is the feeling of what happens when any form of perceiving is going on. It is this particular accompanying feeling that gives rise to our claiming the experience as belonging to us personally as a sense of self.

It seems that our systems are skewed to perceive what is 'out' there in the environment and in a way obscures the internal accompanying bodily and affective sense of self. This, of course, is one of the points that Gibson has also made.[5] Damasio wonders whether in earlier, less complex societies, human beings were naturally more aware of these inner processes of self than we are today.

Emotions and consciousness

Given that consciousness is related to the feeling of what is happening within us, Damasio's radical theory proposes that emotions and consciousness cannot be easily separated. It appears that when consciousness is impaired, so are emotions. People who have had the misfortune to suffer a stroke which has left them profoundly paralysed report no emotional experience to accompany this. It appears that the capacity to feel emotions is linked with the capacity to receive reports about what is happening to our body state. If there are no reports then there are no experiences of emotions.

However, he also distinguishes between emotions and background feelings. Emotions appear to have an evolutionary role in regulating life. They involve complex systems of chemical and neural patterns, which involve a fairly restricted number of subcortical areas of the brain starting from the brain stem and moving upwards. The variety of emotional states cause powerful changes in both brain and body landscape which would include the internal milieu, visceral, vestibular and musculoskeletal systems.

Background emotions are more vague and modify behaviour. They could include feeling stressed, edgy, and are detectable by small details of body posture. Damasio describes these in terms of 'speed and contour of movements, minimal changes in the amount and speed of eye movements and in the degree of contraction of facial muscles'. These background feelings are closer to the 'inner core of life' and their focus is more internal than external. He goes on to suggest that 'background feelings are a faithful index of momentary parameters of inner organismic state'.

The central components that are felt as background feelings come from the movements of the smooth musculature in blood-vessels, organs and heart and chest muscle, the chemical constituency that arises around these muscle fibres, and whether the organism is being mobilized towards a particular perceived threat or is in a state of homeostasis.

How do we experience core consciousness?
According to Damasio, consciousness is a flowlike music that is being made up as it goes along. At the same time, a kind of parallel instrumental score is being formed from mental images and these give us an internal and cognitive counterpart to what is unfolding. In addition, there would need to be musical parts to play states of wakefulness, image formation and various emotions – all of which convey the sense of self. Underneath all of this could be scored a kind of ambient mood music. This would be background feeling. From the outside we might notice background feelings being shown in overall body posture, range of motion of limbs relative to the trunk, spatial profile of limb movements, which can be smooth or jerky, speed

of movements, congruence of movements occurring in different body tiers such as face, hands, and legs, and finally, the animation of the *face*.

In speaking, people also show emotional elements through prosody, like the melody in how we stress and phrase language. All the time, the wordless sense of self is coming from the feeling of what is happening, and it is this that will orientate the shape and direction of mental operations. Damasio argues that language has to be based on the non-language idea of what things are, how they are represented in these various dimensions of representations and body states; words and sentences are speaking of what is already known and felt and graspable. We search for the right word to capture what we are already experiencing nonverbally.

The autobiographical self

The core self is only in the here and now. There is also a much more elaborated sense of self within our consciousness of who we are. This autobiographical self results from what Damasio calls the 'residues' from fleeting moments, the accumulations of *dispositional* (from neural patterns) records which are linked to the core sense of self. An elaborated consciousness results from the capacity to learn and retain records of innumerable experiences. These provide a deeper sense of self grounded from a myriad array of now moments. When these are reactivated in awareness, the brain utilizes the same areas of brain that were used in their first perception. Thus each recollection or thought of something known and recorded will also generate core consciousness moments of self in the process of knowing and experiencing again and again. Extended consciousness is able then to go beyond the limits of here in an enormous and infinite way. As we attend to areas of information not present in the immediate external environment, we can access learning and memory records and systems that are also continuously being affected by new consciousness.

Finally, within this model of consciousness Damasio lists what would be unconscious. These would include images to which we do not attend, all neural patterns that have not become images, all dispositions that were acquired but do not become explicit, and all 'hidden wisdom and know-how' that was created in innate homeostatic processes. Several central ideas emerge from this brief survey of embodied approaches to perception and consciousness.

1 The primary ground of knowing

The first is that knowing and consciousness of other, environment and self depends on nonverbal images prior to language which are based on feeling. Whether or not we are conscious of this, our primary perception is rooted in bodily, affective and sensory systems that provide us with a profound ground of references and signals which are accessible to our awareness if we are interested and pay attention. Many therapists utilize this access to imagery and metaphor as a direct way of going into deeper experiential and less conceptual levels of experiencing. Some theories of psychotherapeutic change maintain that this deeper experiential basis of self must be involved.

I would suggest that in our attempt to 'know' our clients, we can only find ways of meeting them through our knowing of ourselves and the ways clients affect us. All these elements are present to us as wordless knowledge, images, sensations, and different dimensions of affective experiencing. While this points to the highly suspect ground of subjectivity, it remains a concrete and specific source of knowing.

While we can utilize structures of meaning and understanding that have been acquired through intellectual condensations of experience, yet we are compelled to re-insert these into the present way of perceiving and experiencing our clients. When we hear clients' words, we always hear them within a situated and embodied flow of interaction which will shape how we hear them and create meaning between us.

2 Our pre-existing dispositions to certain theories will also tend to shape the way we experience and perceive our clients

Varela's and Gibson's work points us to the recognition of how perception is an active process of organizing ourselves in relation to the world and to others.[4,5] Perception is a highly variable procedure for picking up information. It is shaped by our own way of being embedded within an existing relationship with environment and others. In this model of consciousness, knowledge of the person with us in the moment cannot be reduced to single isolated aspects of theory. It is a dynamic, interactional process because the emotional and background feeling aspects are intricately linked into consciousness which is continuously unfolding and affecting both parties. Knowing and discovering are always relational.

There are also automatized areas of 'dispositions' or learned systems of operating that will shape our perception out of our conscious awareness.

3 The role of attention and perception

In light of the spiral link between attention and consciousness, therapists' work of attending is a vital aspect of knowing and discovering. Given that perception alters with differing bodily positions and intentions, it is not surprising that focusing awareness in particular ways yields different experiences of the client. One example is what happens if the therapist more consciously attentionally follows the bodily movement of the client, even perhaps mirroring it. Therapists then discover a more direct sense of the client's experience than they had without this kind of attention or echo. While our sense of self and our perception of other or environment are highly interwoven, the more we can attend to this felt awareness of self and the subtleties of resonance and response to clients, the more clear we may also become about our own dispositions in response.

It could be argued that both therapists and clients are actively engaged in developing another level of consciousness, a capacity to reflect very consciously on experiencing, on levels of awareness previously considered out of consciousness, even unconscious. Through increasing emphasis on the value of the process of relationship, on relatedness, on monitoring the counter-transference, or the 'embodied counter-transference', psychotherapists are becoming increasingly attuned to more subtle, micro-levels of pre-attentive cognition, which are somatically based. This is a way of discovering our perception of self and other prior to conceptualizing into an idea or thought but tangibly and concretely known within our experiencing. The art of our practice is the increasing sensitivity to monitor what is being transacted between ourselves and our clients, the movement to and from, the qualities of space, silence, disturbance and dissonance that are the musical score of the process. This monitoring then has to alternate with conceptual understanding and meaning which can fit with the kinds of experience we are having. This kind of discernment requires very precise attentive skills and familiarity with the experiential background flow within us.

At this stage, then, having explored some of the multifarious dynamic, affective and parallel processes involved in perception and cognition, the question raised is how and whether awareness of such implicit knowing can be facilitated by meditation or attentional procedures.

The opening quotation to this chapter was written by Swami Vivekenanda.[1] In the context of Raja Yoga, it is suggesting that micro-levels of attention to what is happening can only be developed through meditational kinds of practice. In the next chapter, I move on to consider how meditational practice can facilitate psychotherapy. This will be explored from the perspective of the practitioner's capacities both to attend and to direct attention intentionally to focus awareness in specific ways. It will also be considered from a relational perspective in how changes in the therapist's mode of being may affect the client's own way of experiencing during the session.

3 The Art of Attending – Meditation and Psychotherapy

Introduction

In the previous chapters contemporary approaches to intersubjectivity, perception and consciousness have been explored in order to consider how we may know ourselves and others through a basic ground of sentience and feeling. This much more subtle basis of experience requires more perceptual acuity to cognize what is going on within us. How then can we increase our attentional skill and what difference would it make anyway to our clients?

In this chapter, I will report on how different psychotherapeutic practitioners have found meditation helpful to their work. Different kinds of meditational and attentional styles of focus will be outlined and related to the psychotherapeutic process.

The eye of contemplation

The ancient practices of meditation and contemplation within different spiritual traditions have always offered methodologies for considering the processes involved in perception, and thus the processes involved in the subjective construing of the world. This 'eye of contemplation' is an approach that focuses attention inwardly on experiencing in deliberate and disciplined ways so that extraneous stimuli are restricted and the mind is encouraged to focus on the mental process itself rather than the contents of its workings. Such a methodology provides knowledge which may be more accurately termed *gnosis* – it is a direct knowledge rather than a knowledge about experience – one stage removed into theory or abstraction. Contemporary analysts and researchers maintain that meditation allows a kind of deconstructing of conceptual forms so that the rawer perceptual elements are more foregrounded.

Psychotherapists and meditation

Within much of the literature relating to meditation and psychotherapy, a good deal of interest has been focused on the way therapists attend to their clients and how this can be enhanced and clarified by the consideration of different attentional practices adopted within different meditational systems. The quality of attention within psychotherapy has been given a special role right from Freud's early dictum to adopt an 'evenly suspended attention'.[1] Bion proposed an attention which held neither 'memory nor desire'. Within a phenomenological perspective rooted in yogic traditions by Husserl, a similar dictum was given to provide equal weight to all aspects of the field – the principle of horizontalization.[2] The capacity to attend is intrinsic to the early Greek origins of the word 'therapy'.

As therapists, this reflective capacity to be aware of what we are experiencing is a primary tool in our work and cannot be provided through intellectual means. How we then reflect on the reflection may, however, draw on theoretical ideas and therapeutic models. But the recognition of the power of attending within different foci is a significant aspect of the process of accompanying the client. Recently, many therapists from a range of different therapeutic modalities have reported on the value of meditational practice, and in particular Buddhist practice in their work as therapists (e.g. Welwood,[3,4] Crook and Fontana,[5] Epstein,[6] Coltart[7]). A significant support for practising therapy is to become more acquainted with perceptual procedures which do not require conceptualization and which can facilitate openness and attending. These are the domain of meditation and aesthetic activity. In this mode, a quality of freely hovering attention, of being suspended, of receptivity, of spaciousness can be cultivated which is more facilitative of really attending to what is; to facilitating a genuinely phenomenological attitude. A variety of therapists from many modalities have recognized the value of meditation in assisting therapeutic perception and attention.

What is meditation?

Meditation as a general concept is designed to facilitate the stilling or focusing of mental activity. This may be achieved by focusing attention on one thing such as a candle flame, a word, an idea or an image. As the mind becomes more absorbed within the one focus, the meditator tends to feel the boundaries between self and object as blurred. This kind of meditation is called *concentrative*. It has been found that subjects practising this kind of meditation tend to screen out of awareness other extraneous stimuli. They become absorbed in a kind of flow.

By contrast, a different way of focusing attention is to follow breathing and to allow attention to be directed towards whatever comes into awareness without exercising judgement or involvement. An attitude of simply watching and observing the continual flux of mental process and awareness is adopted. One is attempting to bring the mind into synchrony with its activity rather than darting randomly from awareness to ideas, to memories. Simply watching what emerges in awareness as it happens pulls the subject into the present in a vivid and alert way. This kind of meditation is called *bare attention* or *mindfulness*. The scope of attention is a lot broader and more encompassing than the concentrative kind of awareness. It results in different effects in research.

There are many different kinds of meditation. Meditation simply means resting the mind on one thing. Naranjo and

Ornstein made a distinction between practices that involve 'turning off' awareness, and practices that 'open awareness' up.[8] These are related to processes directed towards disidentifying, identifying through immersion and concentration in an inner way and a third way towards expression, surrender, freedom. Rowan revised this schema into one which categorizes practice according to introverted or extraverted attention directed towards objects.[9] However, Naranjo and Ornstein also stressed that these kinds of distinctions may be an overly schematic way of categorizing a multitude of practices which may in fact interpenetrate rather than be separate. Within particular traditions, both kinds of practice may be employed at different times. Some research has been carried out on Zen and Yogic practitioners. Subjects were exposed to repeated noise. Yogic practitioners who were using concentrative practices which facilitate withdrawal of attention from sensory information showed little EEG responses to the noise. Zen practitioners showed continued EEG responsiveness to repeated sound whereas non-meditators showed an habituation to the noise. The Zen practitioners thus appear to demonstrate the effect of a practice which focused on awareness as it occurs now.[10]

Attentional focus and psychotherapy practice

Kathleen Speeth has recognized that therapy requires different aspects of attention similar to different kinds of meditation.[11] Concentrative kinds of meditation require a narrow focus. Mindfulness kinds of meditation require a more open, receptive wide-angle lens of attention. A further aspect of attention in therapy is being able to direct attention voluntarily from one object to another. The therapist needs to be able to move from outward focus on the client's experience back to her own inner flow of experiencing in parallel with the client.

Nina Coltart emphasized that the use of 'bare attention'

absolutely has to be the scaffolding of everything else that we do. Even when we are doing nothing (or appear to be), sitting in silence, testing our faith in the process – our constant, perhaps I should say only attitude is one of bare attention. It requires a persistent vigilance to train ourselves to observe, and watch, and listen, and feel, in silence ... this kind of attention becomes – second nature. It is the bedrock of our day's work. (p. 181)[7]

How does all of this contribute to working as a psychotherapist? First of all, this capacity to attend and be present allows the therapist to extend an open awareness in a receptive way, to catch the unexpected and to remain more alive to the process. Concentrative kinds of meditation contribute to a capacity to focus on small elements close up in a more persistent and intense kind of scrutiny – a profound attempt to grasp something felt or perceived deeply within the communications of the client.

Beyond the capacity to be more aware, more present, more centred, more focused, meditation enables the capacity to disengage from what is attended to and to take up a different perspective, a reflexive contemplation of how the client is affecting one at the moment or how the in-between of the relationship is progressing.

John Welwood points to a deeper aspect of value for the psychotherapist who meditates.[3,4] The meditator may discover a ground of being that is not conditional on old thoughts or habitual feelings and reactions. Being is grounded in an open space. It allows the therapist to encounter an open ground within, a space of unknowing, a space deeper than constructs and words where the sense of identity is challenged by openness and uncertainty. The capacity to sit with such an openness and unknowing allows a kind of rawness and vulnerability to be felt and shared with the client. When a psychotherapist practitioner is able to apply this kind of attention, Welwood suggests that 'It means being present to what is, facing it as it is, without relying on any view of concept about it' (p. 164).[4]

It does not require any additional 'stuff'; rather a capacity to discover what is there in awareness before the frantic activity of the mental processes has obscured it. Such mental activity has become so identified with our sense of self that to abandon it can be alarming. There appears to be no solidity, no substantiality, no permanence. Welwood points out how this kind of presence with another permits the experiencing of vulnerability and the unknown. This *quality of unconditional presence* is a vital element within potent teachers and healers, he argues. Yet it takes much time and attention to undo the layers of thought and patterning of perception.

Notwithstanding the significance of attention, psychotherapy trainees are rarely given much training in attentional skills. These are provided most thoroughly within the various disciplines of meditation. Terry Lesh showed that Zen meditation improved trainee counsellors' capacity to empathize.[12] How is it then that meditation can facilitate attentional skill as psychotherapists?

The gaps between thought can be breathed through and survived. Winnicott identified primitive spatial agonies of the infant.[13] These are the stuff of falling, coming apart, being annihilated, overwhelmed. Such primitive spatial agonies are often re-experienced or feared within the space offered in a therapeutic session. The therapist's attunement to openness can allow a trust which provides a holding and containing capacity to go through the empty spaces and arrive somewhere. For example, imagine you are in a social gathering; contrast the experience of being held by consistent attention of your listener as opposed to being distracted by another listener's susceptibility to other stimuli. The latter situation creates a sense of being in a scattered and fragmented environment.

From the client's perspective, when a therapist has become more accustomed to resting attention in the present moment, it appears to provide a qualitative different sense of his or her presence. Presence is to do with the present-centred availability of the person. The more this is whole-hearted and engaged, the more the client will feel a field of compassionate spacious possibility in which to explore.

This is both extraordinarily subtle and powerful. Even the slightest difference in attention and presence will result in very different effects of working within a therapeutic process. Even when attention is slightly more sharp and attuned to the client, the resulting understanding will change and the client will feel more met. Without apparent reason, and perhaps on only a very few occasions, I have found the quality of my attention to be of some extraordinarily pristine and profound quality. The whole sense of the therapeutic session has been of a dimensional difference in how the meeting has felt and resonated between us.

Underlying functional approaches to psychotherapy is a much deeper mystery. This is the mystery of understanding of another, the mystery of communication, of how one person can assist another and of how change can happen. Some kind of faith in the possibility of relationship, of something developing, evolving, of something creative being possible, is the only sustaining ground for therapists to stand on. Yet it is a ground that is constantly undermined and giving way. Despite what we believe or consider we understand about psychotherapy, something can work and happen. It is this something that compels so much theorizing and explaining after the event.

Staying with the unknown

The 'bottom–up' view of information processing describes, as we have seen in the previous chapter, the very process of learning and shaping experience before it has been named or categorized and is simply raw dimensions of feeling and experiencing. Inevitably, we are programmed to form new schemas and to integrate patternings so that our brains will work more efficiently and automatically. Nevertheless, it is this area of preconceptual experiencing which is fundamental to being open and present in the moment. It requires an attitude of not-knowing and a willingness to face uncertainty and fear of the new or unfamiliar. It is evidently this area that is developed through meditational practice.

The tension for all therapists is to manage to relate to each person as a unique individual, yet to support their courage with knowledge of theory which is based on generalizations and recognized patterns of recurrent themes and relationships. The old split between mind and body is recast into an arena of conscious and implicit awareness. It is this background awareness that is identified with our sense of ongoing self. It is this base of awareness or emergent self that is the ground for meditation, where mental activity is focused on its own content.

Attention as forming awareness

From a different field entirely, Rudolf Laban (quoted in North[14]) derived a language of movement to describe how people relate to the physical givens of life – how people demonstrate different attitudes to weight, time, space and flow. This way of describing movement creates a phenomenological tool for capturing complex dimensions of embodiment. Each of the 'effort' factors can be yielded to or resisted or may remain as a background dynamic. Marion North elaborates on how these understandings of movement patterns can be applied to psychotherapy in her work *Personality Assessment through Movement*.[14]

- *Weight* represents the 'what' of perception/intention and is related to intentionality, willpower, sensation (responsiveness), the vertical plane and presentation/presence.
- *Space* is related to attention, the 'where', inner attitudes of paying attention and flexibility of attention, mental activities of thinking, and ability for patterning and organization; also horizontal plane and communication.
- *Time* is related to the 'when' aspects of duration, decision-making and intuition. It relates to the how of responsiveness

and aliveness, which can shift or stay the same and it operates in the sagittal plane.
- *Flow* is related to the 'how', precision, emotional feeling and relationships fluency, withholding, continuity.

Any activity usually utilizes three of these effort factors. A person often manifests only two of these habitually and such 'incomplete efforts are indicative of inner attitudes'.

In this context, attention is linked with the factor of space. It is where we put ourselves. Dancers clearly show where they are by their gaze, position of head and focus of attention. When this is altered the whole meaning of the sequence is very different. For example, if attention is directed upward, it will convey a very different sense of meaning than if it is directed downward.

The domain of attention or relation with space can combine with different attitudes towards time, weight and flow. Marion North identified thirty-six different kinds of attentional attitude which included more exaggerated degrees.[14]

For example, combined with the factor of time, attention becomes focused on action, and is a decisive kind of attending. Think of what happens if you are delayed at an airport and then you are waiting to hear that your plane is ready to board. It could be an alert, pin-pointed type of attention ready for action. Alternatively, it could be a more sustained direct attention so that it could be held focused on one task over time, such as is needed when painting a door. It could be an alert and flexible kind of attention able to make quick adaptations across a wide field at the same time. This kind of attention might be needed by a teacher in a large class. It could be a sustained, flexible kind of attention, able to retain a continuing and systematic awareness of a wide field of action, an all-round consideration. This might be needed by a person chairing a very large meeting. It may be that any one of these could become sedimented into a fixed pattern with more negative inferences. It could result in an overly alert focused kind of attention which would convey a sense of expectation, for example. Any one of these could occur within a therapeutic session both in response to what is happening and from the focus of the therapist. It is also evident that each of us would already express certain aspects of these styles intrinsically, and in this way we tend to create a particular ambience or space in which our clients find themselves.

When linked with weight, attention could be direct, pinpointed with a strength of purpose, it could be sensitive, light-touch attention, it could be all-round broad attention with strong concentration on all aspects, it could be sensitive, all-round attention which is unobtrusive. Since weight is related to the experience of presence, any one of these would be felt as particular qualities of relationship, or of intimacy and contact. If we are engaged with others, we often tend to lean forward, put our whole weight into the situation, show commitment and involvement. When we are not so engaged or committed we may lean back, space out, be less connected with our sense of immediate presence or weight.

When combined with flow, attention may be direct, bound and controlled step by step; it could be direct free-flow, deep and far-seeing within a limited area, it could be flexible and bound, with a controlled attention to a wider range of varied aspects, it could be flexible and free-flow, broad and varied, open to impressions and far-seeing. Here the theme is more one of control or spontaneity and freedom. Within the therapeutic relationship these aspects may reflect how we or our clients attempt to control the flow of the session, how much there is a mutual flow, or how much the session allows a deepening of experiential process and expansion of feeling and meaning.

If we apply this kind of mapping of attention within the therapeutic sphere, we may have a more precise way of identifying attention and intention and relationship with others. Since this is a mapping based on movement, it is fundamentally based on intention and perception. What are also conveyed within these brief descriptions are different kinds of knowing and responding that occur from different attentional patterns. They will also arise as a reflection of the content of a client's narrative and the style of relationship that has been forged. Each attentional style is likely to evoke specifically different kinds of responses, and vice versa.

Phenomenologically, our mode of attending and perceiving has the effect of sculpting different domains or territories of experiencing. As therapists, we embody an infinite array of such domains and territories, as do our clients. Where we can meet depends either on the kind of resonance or correspondence we can find within the texture and rhythm of the other's world. Alternatively, there may be times when we mirror a hidden opposite domain that is more implicit within the communication. For example, a client describes a traumatic experience as if it is something that can be thrown away lightly. The therapist may respond by embodying a sensitive, and closely present (weighted) kind of attention which conveys a more feeling response to the event.

Attention as environmental affordance

I would propose that attention can be seen as a kind of environmental affordance from the perspective of Gibson.[15] For Gibson, our environment offers 'affordances' which are different kinds of organismic relationships. Neither object nor subject is prioritized; they exist in mutual relationship. They are discerned primarily through changes of texture. This notion could be applied by considering the kind of affordance that different forms of attention offer. So it is interesting to consider the therapist and her attention as providing a kind of affordance, a kind of environment that has a range of spatial and textural shapings and responses to the client. Christopher Bollas has described the mother and therapist as providing a transformational object experience during development.[16] Such a concept combines the notion of spaciousness and openness so valued by Buddhist practitioners as therapists with a sense of contact and meeting.

Combining different kinds of attentional focus

Kathleen Speeth also adopts the distinction between focused concentrative kinds of attention within the psychotherapeutic work which facilitate identification and empathy compared with those that demand a witnessing, panoramic attention.[11] Attention here is equally directed towards all things. She describes how it seems to lead to 'a feeling of impartiality, spaciousness and breadth of vision' (p. 151). Yet in order to fulfil such a seamless flow of awareness a parallel vigilant attention has to be directed towards maintaining it – which is a kind of concentrated attention. This has been described within a Zen practice quoted from Suzuki Roshi: 'When you are practising Zazen meditation, do not try to stop your thinking'.

Speeth compares this injunction with Freud's instructions to patients in free associating. A third component is the witnessing part of attention that can attend to the flux of events. Speeth's model of therapeutic attention involves all three elements. The panoramic style of attending surveys what is going on in a more external way; the concentrative kind is involved with a deeper, inner kind of affective identification with the other; the third kind allows the therapist to be aware of what she is aware of, to disengage and switch from one mode to another.

Experiments

I have worked with trainees in seminars and in workshops with psychotherapists applying different kinds of intentional attention and presence in practice sessions. Feedback seems to show how different kinds of feelings and images and understandings of the client occur with different kinds of attention or intentions. A more focused attention will tend to create more sense of mergence between therapist and client. Bare attention will tend to create a sense of space and receptivity and safety. Attention directed to both the ground and figure of the client's presence appears to contribute to a greater flow of intuitive imagery and insights about the client. Another way of attending is to gather attention within the heart to listen to another. Here, therapists have reported a sense that they are picking up more of the main feelings within the communications of the other, more of the essence; they feel more connected. It also depends to what extent the notion of listening or seeing through the heart can be evoked in the therapist's approach.

Heart-centred approach
The domain of a heart-centred meditative approach offers another aspect to attention. Rather than being focused on a more visual and 'mindful' quality, heart-based meditation is focused on feeling. Paul Pearsall calls it 'cardio-contemplation'.[17] In focusing attention on the heart, it permits an openness to a natural resonance with all the energies of the present moment, 'thereby expanding, freezing, or spiritually pausing to allow one's self to be completely immersed in the present quantum moment' (p. 155).

Pearsall argues that this kind of meditation is experienced as:

> less private and more connective, more energetically rhythmic than mentally focused and static, and more attentive and receptive to the body's signals than distracted from them ... one tunes into the delicate ... sensations that seem to come from the heart, rather than a word, sound, breathing or image that can be experienced as coming from a consciousness somewhere in the brain. (p. 155)[17]

In conclusion, psychotherapists provide different ways of attending to their clients. Attention appears to offer a reciprocal field of relationship and to subtly alter the quality and style of relational processes. Within any therapeutic session, the therapist needs to focus attention in different ways towards the client, towards her own awareness of being with the client and on the in-between. Certain kinds of preparation facilitate attention. These involve letting go of current mental preoccupations and allowing a more open and experiential awareness of being. Clients appear to pick up the effect of attention and to feel different levels of being held, met or validated by attention. This area is worthy of much further research.

So far, we have looked at the subtle processes going on in relationships, in perception and consciousness and in the ways we can pay attention to these processes with our clients. Meditational practices can be a helpful tool in facilitating attentional modes that are conducive to being more present with our clients. They may also provide environmental kinds of qualities in which a person's experience may be allowed to breathe freely without intrusion. However, attention is not an impersonal capacity; it is rooted within our own personal presence. When attention is linked with a heart-centred focus, it facilitates further aspects of awareness and fellow feeling. It appears to offer us a deeper basis for knowing another person. In the next chapter both perennial and contemporary perspectives of the heart will be discussed.

4 | The Heart as Listener

> When the divine principle moves we feel it as a presence. When you say 'It was a moving experience. The music was moving. His condition was moving. I was moved by his love for me' what is this moved? It is precisely the stirring of the divine principle in the heart which for a moment comes into action. (p. 35)[1]

> [The heart] is the abode of the vital forces, the mind and the light of consciousness.[2]

> A person of heart is someone who is primarily concerned with the cultivation of qualities and meaning.... The Sufi aspires to live in this boundless heart-space. (p. 78)[3]

> The heart can be understood as the totality of qualitative, subconscious faculties, which function in a unified way. (p. 81)[3]

The heart is a mystery

The notion of heart has always been ambiguous – both concrete and spiritual. As a physical organ it represents life and death. As an emotional centre it is where we seem to feel the actual pain of loss and grief. As a spiritual centre it is the seat of the soul. The heart-beat is life in essence. The pulse of our life is what creates the fundamental sense of rhythm and of continuity, despite fluctuation. It is possible that the heart provides a temporal template for the infant to organize patternings among the different sensory modalities. This cross-modal capacity is a crucial basis for metaphor and language, like Aristotle's original term of 'common sense'.[4] Within spiritual traditions, the heart holds a pivotal place between physical and divine realms; it is the place of soul and of intuition. Within the Sufic tradition there are layers within the heart, and in the core centre of the heart is essence – the heart of hearts, innermost source of knowledge and wisdom.

Within contemporary discourse *heart* is primarily a medical phenomenon. Now televisually familiar in surgical documentaries, its pulses and quivering visceral vitality inform our sense of life and death. In the same way that the shock of the Earth seen from outer space has transformed our sense of this planet, the sight of a heart removed from situ, being mended while a patient is kept alive by a mechanical pump, has transformed our relation with the heart, previously felt and known as an essential fluttering and percussive base of continuity safe within the depths of our chest cavity. Imagine that a primary schema or structure of thinking in relation to body experiences is one relating to containment. Johnson, for example, proposes that 'our encounter with containment and boundedness is one of the most pervasive features of our bodily experience' (p. 21).[5] Perhaps, then, this literal dislocation of heart is a resonant symbol of the pervasive sense of dislocation which is common to our times. For it appears to be a fundamental aspect of our experience of ourselves and of our heart that it is inside us in a core/coeur way.

We know, however, that the heart can be fixed and worked on from outside so that life may continue and flourish. Just to say the word *heart* instantly evokes a database of biological mechanisms and medical associations. The threat of the heart attack subtly pervades our daily prescriptions for diet and exercise and lifestyle. It is a common human experience to have had some kind of closer exposure to the exigencies of heart malfunctioning and failing among our families and friends. So it is both the fundamental measure of life, yet fragile and capable of being sorted out by more knowing and expert figures. It is the source of our life with all the depth of meaning that is implied and yet it is frequently reduced to a simple mass of tissue and cells – just a phenomenon of biology, matter, the straightforward procedures involving the knife, bypassing blocked tubes, attaching an external source of maintenance – making pace.

Any of the above sentences may be taken as powerful sources of meaning and metaphor simply because they concern the heart. Within our language structures and metaphors, the heart discloses a rich subjective and intersubjective life. The French 'coeur' is touched in English within the notion of 'core' which can be a quality of heart. What is the difference between putting our heart into something and not? Individuals may be described as having big hearts, warm hearts, soft hearts, good hearts, or cold or mean hearts. We can feel faint-hearted, lacking heart, sick at heart. We can be half-hearted. Someone can have a heart of gold, another is black-hearted. Hearts beat stronger throughout all romantic fiction and in life when the significance of persons and situations is known through the heart beating or even missing a beat. Projects and creative efforts can have heart or lack heart. We set our hearts on something. When we want to reach to the quintessence, the core, of anything, we use the word *heart*. Is there a link between heart and hearth? When we gesture with hands towards ourselves, the place where me or I exists bodily, we point instinctively to the heart area. In our heart of hearts is a source of direct and ultimate knowledge, a knowledge of inner, subjective truth that is indisputable despite other sources of information or opinion.

What is disclosed by these kinds of metaphor about the heart? What appear to be conveyed are some particular dimensions of being *and feeling* that can be put into living in certain ways. The metaphors suggest aspects of intention, integration, knowledge, space and attunement. So the question arises as to whether it is possible to talk of feeling or sense of self as heart? Whether it is possible to regard the increasing recognition of the implicit, the pre-attentional cognition, the primacy of feeling or perception as to do with the embodied field of feeling, background awareness, gathered and synthesized temporally in patterns by the heart-beat, by the centre of being.

The heart within perennial philosophy

Blessed are the Pure in Heart for they shall see God.

From the perspective of the perennial spiritual traditions, the heart is the centre of being, the centre of body, mind and soul and an opening to the divine. The heart itself as a chakra or spiritual centre can provide a sentience-like perception. It is through this sentience and its refinement that the spiritual aspects within a person may be felt and glimpsed. For those involved in spiritual practice, particularly one that involves the heart centre, a central aspect to develop perception within the heart is that of purification or cleansing of its lens. The Sufis describe the process as *tuning* the heart. Like an instrument, the heart's capacity to resonate truly may be distorted by the influence of many other dissonances. Another metaphor is that of polishing the mirror. The mirror of our self-experiencing becomes clouded by sedimentations and delusions so that our perception is also clouded.

In purifying the heart centre, an openness to experiencing is increased as is an openness to compassion. The development of perception within spiritual practice is to refine a specific kind of knowing – based more on feeling than thinking, because it is less constrained by concept. For the mystic's quest to know the divine cannot be based on intellectual process.

It is the same for the therapist, since he or she cannot 'know' the client through intellectual concepts, although it would often appear that this is what therapeutic training requires. As Jung said, we do not do well to look at the sky with the intellect; nor is it adequate for the knowledge of the psyche.[6]

In Sahaj Marg meditation, the heart is also gradually purified of background impressions which restrict perception and cognition so that there is a clearer field of experiencing/feeling.[7] This results in more and more sensitivity to the feelings of others and an increase in capacity for empathy. Whereas the concept of heart is not one that fits neatly into academic discourse, within the perennial philosophies in East and West the heart is regarded as the place of soul, of love, of knowledge and wisdom. Knowledge and wisdom of the heart come through feeling rather than intellectual construct. The spiritual heart which is located more subtly than the physical heart is described as the deeper basis of mind within Yogic, Buddhist and Sufic philosophies. The 'Sacred Heart' within Christian mysticism would also echo the notion of the heart as a central place of organization within the human system. It is not only a physical centre, but one that links the connection with the spiritual to the human.

Ram Chandra, the teacher of a modern form of Raj Yoga called Sahaj Marg, wrote: '[the heart] is the field for the mind to work, and this is the instrument by which we develop the discriminating faculty'.[7] From this perspective, the heart may be compared with the entire field of awareness arising from our embodiment in the world. The heart is a gathering place for the mind to focus its interpretation of this ground.

Within the perennial philosophies, the capacity to integrate awareness into a core understanding is one that has also been named as concerning the heart. More explicitly within the Yogic and Sufic traditions, the heart is understood to be an organ of subtle perception that integrates all perceptual systems. As a membrane of a gathered comprehensive perception, it requires cleansing since it tends to be clouded with the residues of myriad more surface attractions and distractions. If it is 'polished' by attention to the narrow preoccupations of the ego, the heart can then act as a mirror. It can discern and reflect qualities.[3] It is suggested within Sufic philosophy that qualities are a primary manifestation of existence. The polished heart can reflect qualities which we find more meaningful in human existence, love, compassion, sharing, peace, a deeper sense of relatedness as well as other qualities of infinite variation. Therefore, in this sense, the heart is capable of discriminating tiny changes and fluctuations within experiencing that are involved with different qualities of feeling.

Common to many spiritual traditions is the work of penetrating the layers of distortions in perception that obscure inner direct knowledge. The impact of external impressions is understood to create attachments to material objects and to hide inner perceptions of realities that can be perceived by 'inner perceptual organs' within the mind rather than those operating at a sensory and physical level. The role of the heart in this process is a pivotal one because it is situated in the place between physical and spiritual domains. The heart carries the impressions of experience.

Within yoga, the focus of effort is to refine perception so that it may observe in a more dispassionate way the inner realms of perception. This process requires an awareness of how feeling and willing affect cognition:

> In yoga, impossible though it may seem, an attempt is made to exclude error from the thought-life, in order to think objectively. A thorough purging of the whole individual is required in respect to the entire psychic structure. Because thinking, feeling and willing interpenetrate one another, it is of little use to clarify and cleanse the thoughts, if ... impulses ... arise ... again.... In the sub-conscious resides everything.[2] (p. 75)

Within the different subtle centres or chakras lies the heart (Anahata) chakra. This is described as a twelve-petalled lotus – heart chakra anna means grace, and within it lies a smaller eight-petalled lotus – inner shrine of worship of God which is red.

> Anahata also means 'unstruck sound' in Sanskrit. This fourth chakra is associated with air as an element. It is the place where mind and body meet. The conception of balance is therefore pivotal in allowing the source of love, within the soul, to be manifest. The 'unstruck sound' refers to the origin of creation, of sound, of vibration, the original sound not produced by friction. Therefore it requires fine tuning for this sound to be played, a removal of dis-

torting layers. In poetry, this is described as celestial music, flowing from the divine playmate of humanity, Krishna.[8]

There are six virtues identified which need to be cultivated in order to open this centre. These include the interpretation of incoming impressions in a symbolic or analogical way as well as cultivating consecutive logical thought processes, controlling actions, developing perseverance, tolerance, empathy, confidence and faith and openness to everything, and a capacity to keep a sense of proportion – a balanced attitude in all conditions of life. Balance here again reflects the notion of heart as a pivotal centre between body, emotions, intellect and spirit.[7]

Apparently also, and intriguingly, Yoga doctrine sees a relationship between the twelve-petalled lotus and the sense of touch. The organ of this sense is the skin which covers the entire periphery of the body. Thus touch is indeed the most peripheral of the senses. Its opposite pole is a centring activity in the heart. The ego is like the centre of the circle. This connection between feeling, skin and heart is an interesting one in the light of the work of Candace Pert[9] and others who show how emotion and perception are distributed throughout the body in neuropeptides interacting with nodal points linking with the brain. Touch also appears to be a primary perceptual experience, the basis of kinaesthetic orientation and crucial to the survival of infants.

Heart as source of intelligence

The Sufi mystic, Hazrat Inyhat Khan[10] anticipated some aspects of the work of Antonio Damasio[11] when he wrote that mind and feeling are the same:

> Feeling is a deeper aspect of mind. In other words, we do not have to struggle to assert mind over feeling, nor treat these as entirely separate domains of subject and object, but as two mutually informing and intertwining aspects of living.

In Sufic literature, the heart is often defined and considered as a divine subtlety attached to the physical organ of the heart, and it is that subtlety which holds the truth within man.[11] Within the centre of our bodied and spiritual selves the heart is both physically and spiritually located. It is maintained that the heart provides the means for transformation through perception and consciousness. The heart has no limit to its expansion or understanding and this constitutes a *heart informed* intelligence. Comprehension and understanding are directly related to the heart. The brain is only a further means or auxiliary by which comprehension takes place.

Heart in Arabic is *qalb*, which means turning or revolving. The heart turns if it is functioning properly and will then not fix or attach to anything. There is only dynamic orientation, equilibrium and connectedness in flux – a primal, unific experience. In this sense the heart is like radar, the heart transmits and receives signals. It can be fixed in one direction – for example, in emotional attachment and possessiveness towards a child – or it can be 'attuned' to spiritual aspiration.[3]

> The definition of the heart is that it is the depth of the mind, the mind being the surface of the heart.... It is the same thing which thinks and feels, but the direction is different: feeling comes from the depth, thought from the surface. (p. 172)[12]

The psychic structure was understood to consist of five internal senses: common sense, imagination, intelligence, memory and active imagination or intellect.

> Common sense is understood as the ability to perceive the forms of things, whereas imagination is the ability to perceive meanings; when one has perceived both form and meaning, both these psychic structures are operative. Intelligence is the ability to preserve forms and memory is the ability to preserve meanings. These two functions play a very important role in contemplation. The fifth psychic structure is known by many names: it is the intu-

itive ability to govern both sensible phenomena and intelligible noumena so that a balance is always preserved. Sufis call it the spiritual heart. (pp. 19–20)[13]

Within Sufic literature the metaphor of the Garden of Paradise was used to convey four stages of the mystic journey – Garden of Soul, Garden of Heart, Spirit, and Essence.[13] The soul has to gather the inner senses or the faculties of intuition and to penetrate beyond forms to a direct knowledge. The famous work by Farid Ud-Din Attar entitled *The Conference of the Birds* describes this process.[14] The birds are symbolic of different faculties of perception. Only those faculties which have been awakened to the inner aspect of things, and which can see beyond materiality, choose to make the journey towards completion. Others, for example, the nightingale, cannot make the journey because they are caught in the external form of things; likewise the duck cannot leave water, the hawk cannot leave its prey.

The notion of the heart's centre is that to which desire is directed – in other words it is a primary basis of orientation or attunement. A. H. Almaas, a former psycho-analyst and current teacher and practitioner in the Diamond Heart path, also describes a centre within the heart at a deeper level below the heart chakra.[15] This is one of the centres that the Sufis call *lataif*. These centres are sometimes called 'organs of perception'. In the heart it is connected with the experience of compassion. Heart may be used as essence, indicating the presence of true nature in all its facets.

Another Sufi teacher, Shaykh Haeri, defines the rational self as one that perceives all events which can be perceived through the senses at once and can judge them accordingly.

> For within the rational self there is a common denominator of sensing. It is called the unifying sense (we normally refer to it as the common sense) because it has the ability to integrate at once all the various bits it senses.[16]

Another way of describing this is to relate and connect all awarenesses and understanding to the heart, implying that the brain relates to the heart. Comprehension and understanding then are directly related to the heart. The brain is only a further means or auxiliary by which comprehension takes place. This view pin-pointing the heart as the centre of cognizances is also included in the Quaran/Bible.

> Have they not travelled in the land so that they should have hearts with which to understand, or ears with which to hear? For surely it is not the eyes that are blind, but blind are the hearts which are in the breasts.

The heart in psychotherapy

Heart is the best metaphor I can find to use as a relational matrix for orientation, awareness and interconnection. The heart reflects the subjective inner experiencing based on feeling and also that aspect of self that is most touched by the experience of others, is intrinsically relational. It appears to be both a metaphor for that which is most central within us and that which is most accessible to others and the world. Even within our secular times, *heart* is still a term that occupies an ambiguous ground between archetype, physical life centre, metaphysical entity. Within some contemporary neuroscientific research, it appears that the heart may also possess physical characteristics that place it more centrally within the processes of mind/body. It is essentially still mysterious. However, for the purposes of this work, the heart is a way of capturing the place of intention in relation to the other and the place of feeling, intuition, thought and reflection.

Heart and attention

Focusing attention through the heart allows a different kind of contact to be made with others. It is the source of direct knowing, as opposed to knowing *about* that comes through the mental process of categorization and conceptualization of experience. Another way of considering this is to link it with the notions of consciousness that have been proposed here or the related ways of describing – implicit relational procedures, the felt sense, the unthought known – all of which describe the way we can be in touch with something in another person through feeling rather than words *per se*. Our perceptual systems are geared towards monitoring the effect of every moment on our experiencing. Bodily experiencing is the way the brain minds the body. The capacity to translate sensory modalities requires the capacity to perceive temporal flux in information and to compare rhythms and phrasing that link speech with vision, touch with vision, and so on. Aristotle formulated the concept of 'common sense' to propose the heart's capacity to integrate experience. Within perennial philosophy, the heart plays this role of integrator of experience.

If the heart is at the centre of physical existence, it is possible to construe (as Gary Schwartz and associates have done, according to Pearsall[16]) that the energy transmitted to and from the body's complex systems is also a way of transmitting information back and forth. In this way, the heart can be seen as a primary source of attunement and connection with the experiencing response of the body at a visceral and subtle level.

As we have seen, mystics have perceived the heart as a bridge between the material and the spiritual realms of existence. As the basis of consciousness as feeling it presents an infinite capacity to pick up and attend to others. One of the roots of the word *tolerance* comes from the notion of allowing space for the other to exist. It seems that we can allow others the space to exist more from heart than head.

Contemporary perspectives on heart

More recent perspectives on how we operate from moment to moment have stressed a recognition that the notion of what is mind is something that includes body and feeling. In *Descartes' Error* (1994) Damasio investigated how emotion is inextricably linked into reasoning and decision processes.[17] Feeling is a basis for thinking and deciding and part of the information will come from the response of the heart.

Gary Schwartz of the Human Energy Systems Laboratory at the University of Arizona proposes that the heart is involved with communicating information and energy since energy and information are intrinsically linked.[16] Since the heart communicates with all the cells within the system, it is involved in a considerable gathering and sending out of information with each beat. This field is called *cardio-energetics*. An experiment was carried out between two people who sat opposite each other in a room. Separate ECGs and EEGs were attached to both and were measured at the same time. Initial results showed that each person's heart appeared to transmit energy to his or her brain. It then appeared that one person's heart exchanged energy with the other person's brain. There also appeared to be an exchange of energy between both individuals' hearts. This was in the form of some kind of resonating effect – like tuning.

Candace Pert's work on neuropeptides has demonstrated how the process of thinking and responding is shaped by information from neurotransmitters and neuropeptides as they are distributed throughout bodily systems.[9] They are actively involved in stimulating complex responses through the nervous system. The nervous system is not only organized by the brain and by neural circuitry but also through chemistry which links together body/mind processes – including heart and gut.

Chilton Pearce[18] reported on research carried out through the National Institute of Mental Health[19] that the heart provides an ongoing report of the environmental situation to the brain 'exhorting' the brain to make an appropriate response. The heart contains a hormonal transmitter that also plays a vital role in cognitive processes and particularly in relation to the limbic part of the brain. Within the atrium of the heart, there is a hormone called ANF which determines the activities of the thalamus and its link with the pituitary gland. This is the gland which controls the whole endocrine system. The hormone ANF is involved in the healing response of the body and the immune system. Since it affects the hypothalamus and pineal gland and their production of melatonin, this hormone within the heart then plays an important role in relation to stress, memory and learning, according to Pearce. There is an afferent pathway which originates from the heart's own 'intrinsic nervous system' that links to the brain through the spinal cord. The heart has its own intrinsic nervous system which operates and processes information independently of the brain or nervous system. This is why heart transplants can work even while nerve connections with the spine are being reformed.

Coherence

Researchers at the Institute of Heartmath propose that the heart plays a vital role in integrating cognitive and emotional states. They suggest that the heart transmits information relative to the current emotional state to the cardiac centre of the brain stem. These connect with the thalamus and amygdala which are critical for decision-making and integration of reason and feeling. Signals are sent from here to the rest of the cortex to help synchronize cortical activity. This is why the heart's rhythms can change the coherence in the brainwave pattern and thereby modify brain function. Their research findings indicate that when the heart is sending coherent information to the brain, cortical function and positive feelings are facilitated.

Heart as an oscillator

Another phenomenon that has been observed in heart cells is that they will vibrate in synchrony even if removed and kept separate from each other. Somehow these cells are linked through a field which facilitates this connection – there is a nonlocal mechanism operating here. According to Heartmath, the heart is the strongest known biological oscillator – anything which produces a rhythmic pattern of energy or movement. Within natural systems, oscillators tend to synchronize. Within the body, the heart will tend to entrain other oscillating systems in the body and apparently can entrain other hearts even over distances. Since the rule is that the strongest oscillating field exerts greatest influence over other oscillators, it is claimed that the heart has an electrical field forty to sixty times stronger than the brain and a magnetic field two to 4000 times more powerful than the brain. The heart is thus the central dynamic in setting the frequency patterns of all bodily systems – from the brain to the spin of the blood cells. They propose that thought and feeling are the determining factors in what frequencies are being generated by the heart. Certain more compassionate or calm states of feeling apparently create more coherent and smooth wave forms which tend to bring other oscillators into entrainment. This approach has subsequently been applied to a biofeedback technology which managers have used in improving communication with others. At an informal level of report, it seems to be something significantly useful.

James Lynch researched verbal communication and its effect on blood pressure.[20] He found that vascular changes associated with alterations of blood pressure were related to emotional reactions and heart rate. Talking in everyday conversation increases blood pressure. However, attentive listening decreases blood pressure. If someone listens while thinking what to say next, blood pressure does not decrease; it is only if someone truly sets aside current thinking processes and pays attention to the other that blood pressure decreases.

The Institute of Heartmath has set up an extensive system of biofeedback software and training courses for organizations and individuals, and trains people to intentionally focus attention in the heart and to generate positive feelings. It appears that dramatic physiological changes arise from this. There are increased coherence and rhythmic patterns in the heart, which affect the whole body and brain. The Institute claims all this increases awareness, energy and mental capacity. Intriguing research with patients who have received heart transplants has shown that the patients appear to manifest preferences and tastes and other personality aspects that belonged to the person whose heart has been transplanted. As yet, we do not have adequate scientific models to account for such phenomena.[16]

Chilton Pearce is concerned with the impact that heart-to-heart contact has on mother–child bonding and the initiation of many vital developmental processes in the infant.[18] Proximity to the mother's heartbeat is the major stimulus for the shutdown of the birth-stress hormonal reaction. The separate sensory systems are stimulated by the visual proximity to the mother's face and in feeding.

Three modalities of listening

Some approaches to attention in meditation tend to emphasize a visual modality of space and sky and clarity such as Buddhist practices. This can be because attention is focused outwards and sometimes with the eyes open. Other approaches tend to evoke more feeling or sound emphasis such as Yoga and devotional traditions, perhaps because they are more inner directed. These latter stress either more inner absorption or immersion or focus on heart or love. However, there seems to be a significant difference in gathering such attentional practices within the matrix of heart because it is a way of locating attention within a relational sphere. Instead of meditation for my own perception and awareness, it is a way of directing attention so that I can be more attentive or facilitative towards the other and our interaction together.

In bringing together some of these possibilities of description of attention, of listening from heart, I have deduced three modalities or dimensions of attending that can be provided in listening and involve dimensions of the heart: *attunement*, *amplification* and *depth*. Each of these modalities may arise sequentially within the unfolding of the therapeutic relationship or operate in parallel during one session.

These three modalities are also representative of an arc of contact, arousal and resonance reminiscent of Stern's concept of the vitality contour,[21] or the wordless felt narrative within core consciousness described by Damasio.[11] Each of these modalities is subject to continual modification and refinement over time as with all perceptual systems. These terms therefore offer descriptions for modalities of attention and perception which are intrinsic to relationship at either a very simple or profound level of being in the world.

Attunement
First, the concept of attunement or resonance provides a way of connecting with others. It requires a certain accommodation and sensitivity. Before anything, there is the need to be attuned to oneself. Gendlin's process of focusing is a way of attuning ourselves to the felt sense of being at present.[22] Attunement is a way of directing a kind of felt sense through my heart in relation to the other. I tune into myself listening to the other, listening and perceiving the other such that there is a sense of being in touch, meeting, understanding, resonance. It requires a fine touch and a capacity to focus attention concentratedly and to capture the differing levels of fluctuating information emanating from the other; from the variable patterns a main underlying theme can be felt. How do we tune into another person? It involves following the other's rhythm, phrasing, movement patterns. In the same way that we may wish to join in a dance and have to follow the movement of others and allow their movement to mould ours, a certain level of synchrony has to arise. In the way that mothers synchronize with babies through eye contact and facial expression initially, attunement is a kind of sounding out through oscillating wave forms between two people.

Often in early sessions with clients, it is not easy to achieve this and the process itself can be very tiring. Over time, the repetition of meetings can create its own pattern of synchrony in rhythm and phrasing and in the shapes of narratives that are woven between therapist and client. When this kind of attunement has been sufficiently established, it may be possible to say that this describes what we mean by a working alliance. It allows for more diversity and challenge to alter the key and modalities of the process, more contrasts of dissonance and resonance to be balanced by an overall rhythm and flow. Attunement is also like holding. One therapist talked about holding her client through very difficult material simply by maintaining contact through an attunement in meeting his eyes.

The attuned heart is one that is able to feel and connect with others through matching movement and the indications of inner experiencing that are manifested in many small gestures and rhythms. It seems to penetrate below the surface to an affective level from the beginning. This is why it facilitates a quality of human contact that is not achieved by mental activity and thinking.

Amplification
Second, there is the aspect of expansiveness within the heart domain, a possibility of openness, spaciousness – having a big heart. It requires a letting go of fixed conceptualization or categorization and a certain allowing, accepting, yielding attitude.

It is also something that has spatial characteristics, large and small, wide and deep, encompassing or shrinking from what it encounters. A big heart can manage to sustain contact with painful and difficult circumstances, and can also go beyond pure self-interest. It has a quality of surrounding or absorbing experience so that something can be held and acknowledged at a deeper level rather than denied or rejected.

Depth
The third aspect of attention, perception and intention is that of depth of field. Depth is a quality that appears to be something crucial to subjectivity and meaning; it allows the figure to

be held within a ground that goes beyond immediate temporal and spatial boundaries. Therapists offer a context of space and time that is held constant to support changes and the possibilities of change within the unknowns of time and space. It is the quality of the heart-to-heart kind of knowing; the most meaningful aspects of being alive; a quality of emotional feeling that is absolute, a sense of reaching to the bottom of being, the essence, so that what is background to such figural experience is also expanded dimensionally. It indicates a level of penetration and discrimination as well as a sense of relatedness to the largeness of life.

It relates to the notion of intention *putting heart into something* – the degree of weight or sustained focus we may place on experience and at a profound ontological level commitment to hearing the other's meaning. This conveys a kind of commitment, alignment and integration of all of our capacities that can be surrendered or withheld from persons and situations. This kind of knowledge represents two aspects of knowledge; one is an overall synthesized gathering of felt meaning, experiential and close to a kind of wisdom. The other is more a focused beam of clarity or meaning that penetrates to the essence of a situation or person.

> Depth, this mysterious dimension ... is the first, most primordial dimension, from which all others are abstracted. The primordial experience of depth is always the experience of a sort of interiority of the external world, such that each thing I perceive seems to implicate everything else, so that things, landscapes, faces all have a coherence, all suggest a secret familiarity.[23]

Summary

The heart may be conceived metaphysically, metaphorically, phenomenologically or concretely as a domain of perception and response. It appears to offer at least three possible modalities of focusing our feeling and responsiveness to others. These are aspects of our perception and focus that may be unconscious or may be facilitated by conscious intentional procedures. They may require a capacity to be in tune with ourselves, to relax, to let go of pressing mental processes in order to facilitate a receptivity to the other or to the environment. Another kind of heart attention creates an infinite and receptive quality of acceptance or spaciousness. The third dimension involves a quality of deepening and resonating. All of these also require a capacity to pay ourselves a similar quality of attention.

In the final section of the book, these three aspects of heart listening – attunement, amplification and depth – will be explored further, with examples and exercises to try out.

5 | Attunement: A Relational Sense of Focused Awareness

> There are two aspects of life: the first is that man is tuned by his surroundings, and the second is that man can tune himself in spite of his surroundings. This latter is the work of the mystic.[1]

What is attunement?

Attune means to adjust or accustom oneself to a particular situation (*Oxford Concise Dictionary* 1999). With a musical instrument this involves adjustment to pitch. With television or radio a particular circuit is adjusted to receive transmission of information. With a car engine it can mean the notion of rebalancing so that all the parts run smoothly and efficiently. In human situations attunement is a capacity we use all the time to adjust and adapt to changes of context, meeting, personality, purpose. Within the context of Sufic philosophy, attunement seems to indicate orientation. It involves gathering all one's attention and intention within the heart towards the beloved or sacred source. Attunement then becomes a kind of radar and orientation which serves as a continuous guidance system towards the divine. If we allow all these meanings to play across our sensibilities, it is clear that attunement is a reciprocal process of activity and receptivity which involves a monitoring ear or response to 'fine tune' to an exact fit. The experience of 'exact fit' between two individuals is a sufficiently rare experience to be regarded as special and possessing a quality of deeper meaning and feeling. Much of the time, our daily life is felt to be a series of attempts to adjust or to signal messages to others to attune to with more or less success or dissonance.

Before attunement there was the notion of tune. In this

context, the idea is to focus attention on the essential sound of the person. This involves pitch, tone, volume, form and phrasing. It is defined as *a melody, especially one which characterizes a certain piece of music.* This concept of melody may be particularly resonant in relation to our experience of each other. Movement observers and therapists have found music to be the best analogy to describe the way infants seem to manifest a latent style or being which is perceived in patterns of phrasing within movement schemes.[2,3] Infants demonstrate 'vitality affects' in terms of a sense of enthusiasm and commitment through kicking and waving and overall movement which can alter in intensity and rhythm and phrasing. Any person who has observed new-born infants will notice a considerable range of movement style in this way. This, in turn, might be felt within the level of tonus within the baby's body when held, different qualities of rigidity, flexibility, aliveness, resistance. Movement observers have adopted the term 'moulding' to describe the way babies will accommodate or adjust to the holding body and arms of the carer – and vice versa. An acquaintance who meets many new babies through her work described how she could be sensitive to very different messages of how the baby wanted to be held.

Melody and individual styles of being

So the notion of melody can describe how idiosyncratic styles of movement – sustained moments suddenly shifting into faster, lighter movements – can resemble low notes moving to high notes on a scale. The repertoire can broaden and develop. Within movement observation schemes such as the one Laban (quoted in North) evolved,[3] each of us has many dimensions of movement to play with as embodied beings. We have weight, space, time and flow. We have innumerable internal movements and oscillations occurring within musculo-skeletal structures, internal organs, tiny, smooth muscles in our blood-vessels, the subtle electrochemical transmissions of energy and nation through chemical transmitters and neural networks, and at the base of all of this the steady beat of the heart. As has been noted, the heart is a more powerful oscillator than the brain within the human system. It is claimed that all the other bodily systems become entrained through the rhythm of the heart. These are the melodies and counterpoints that go on within each movement of living.

We all perceive this orchestration of movement and are highly skilled in hearing *sound*s that are emitted in human styles of communicating. If we are trying to recognize someone from a distance beyond clear visual view, it is the characteristic style of movement that will be a more primary recognizable feature than visual features alone. Individuals exhibit a great difference in range – the octaves of melody or movement style may occur within the repertoire of some and not others. For example, some people can sustain much higher levels and intensities of movement and sudden changes in movement than others. This may be contrasted with a style of movement or being which has less variation, is more sustained and even in style and less noticeable.

As therapists, we learn to become accustomed to the melody of each client – the usual way they move and act and speak and the narratives they unfold will all reflect an idiosyncratic melody. Sometimes, it seems as though the client has only very few notes to play in response to the noise of the environment. These few notes then appear to limit the capacity of someone to adapt or respond sufficiently to the changing cacophony which life throws up unremittingly. Then, within any one therapeutic session, it may be that each element within the narrative and dialogue is like a variation on a theme, or may be played in a different key, or may be entirely dissonant or discontinuous with the other phrases in the melody.

Attunement in action

A parent attunes to the infant, not only by mirroring the exact gesture but by capturing the dynamic and affective qualities so that a child's shout may be mirrored by a parallel movement of swooping the child up. As counsellors, we translate the felt sense of a client's experience into something that captures the quality and texture by translating the feel of the communication into our own choice of words that still resonate with the client's experience. We can touch the experience with the client and yet make use of very different words.

In clinical supervision it is also possible to discern a felt sense, an experiential grasp second-hand in a supervisee's reportage, focusing on qualities of movement in how someone makes transitions. Some essential aspect of the client often seems to be conveyed in how he or she negotiates one event and another. When we listen again to these implicit expressions, kinaesthetically, experientially, through the material of life history, we often find a more fruitful source in facilitating a feel of the client than fitting life histories into theory. It is these experiential aspects that are manifest in parallel processing in supervision sessions.

A simple example of this occurs when we observe what has been called 'parallel processing' within supervision sessions. What can often be observed during supervision is the way dynamic patterns of relationship become repeated during supervision.[4] At a closer level, it appears that the dynamic patterns are reflective of flow processes – how the flow between therapist and client can be restricted or unreceptive. I would suggest that these parallel processes are similar to Stern's model of vitality contours. He describes these as being made up of micro-processes of arousal, activation and hedonics occurring during interactions. In movement analysis, these would all contribute to overall flow.

For example, in a recent supervision session in which I worked, the supervisee was bringing the case of a child therapy/play session. His repeated comment was how difficult it was to keep up with the child's sudden switches of activity and how he kept 'missing' him. Within the supervision session, the supervisee's account of the process appeared also to contain a great momentum, and when other members of the group intervened with their understandings and comments, the same dynamic of tension between flow and interpretation or intervention appeared to be happening. It seemed as though the supervisee also felt a strong need to keep going and not be interrupted. From the perspective of attunement in this instance, what became suddenly recognizable was a vitality contour which presented similar dynamic patterns of flow and shifts of flow, and that was how the parallel process was recognized.

In group situations, this kind of multifarious aspect of individuals is obviously more complex. Yet if we reflect on different groupings of people which may occur over time, it appears that each group can also appear to sound a particular tune or melody within which there may be out-of-tune notes and dissonant sub-phrases and awkward orchestrations.

Making a chord from dissonant notes

This became clearer to me recently when I listened to a modern composer's symphony. Certain chords were sounded which covered (to my untutored ear) perhaps five different notes. I was conscious of how these different notes may have been hard to make into one chord, and yet within the composition of musical instruments playing these five notes they appeared to make a chord which held the tension between the dissonances for the time period of the chord played. (It is perhaps an interesting tangential point that our capacity to hear harmony from the combination of different notes has steadily developed over history. Until the eleventh or twelfth centuries thirds and fifths were perceived as dissonant whereas now they are the standard repertoire of composers.[5])

In resonating with the experience of this balance of tension and holding in the chord, I was mostly reminded of attuning either to individuals with degrees of anxiety or frustration or to groups of dissenting people. Something within my heart/chest area seems to stretch wider and to be in touch with each different note. I am bodily conscious of receiving slightly different information whether it is termed sound, feeling, or image or thought. If I am to manage a successful sense of meeting and hearing these dissonances, something has to adjust in me to fit with these slightly out-of-tune margins between different points of view, or different feelings, or different tones of voice. Something in me seems to struggle to make some kind of chord among all the different tonalities. In concrete terms, this would be manifested well by offering a reflective or empathic kind of response in which I showed I had recognized these different elements. If there is enough fit here, it seems as though the melody can continue and unfold and move along.

However, if there is not enough fit, the phrasing can get more stuck or the notes more dissonant. It is possible at this point for the whole melody to become fragmented. A paradoxical example of this occurred with one client whom I have worked with. The story or tune that repeated in her narrative was one which in fact had never been listened to or played by others. Whenever I attempted to pick up resonances within her discourse, they did not fit with this tune which was one of dissonance. Thus over time, until I was able to recognize this darker, less audible accompaniment to the main tune, we could not make a fit. Until I was able to play back the more familiar dissonances in her meetings with others, and with me, we could not make any kind of chord or meeting place between us. It seems that as therapists we need to be able to attune to dissonance which is much less comfortable than resonance.

Stern's discussion of affect attunement

In Chapter 1, Stern's work on infant development was outlined in terms of the intersubjective process.[6] As part of this process, he describes an attunement as a 'recasting, a restatement of a subjective state' (p. 161). In researching communication between mothers and infants he observed how mothers appear to match the tunes their infants play. There is a crucial and subtle distinction to note between the idea of matching as opposed to mirroring or imitating. The mother manages to catch the intensity, time and shape of a movement from the baby – whether facial expression, sound, gesture or combination.

Changing from mirroring to recasting inner experience

It was noticed that until about nine months, mothers tended to respond at first within the same sensory modality as the baby's original communication. Once echoed back, the mother would introduce a theme and variations based on the original gesture or sound. However, after nine months, it appears that mothers may initiate matching through corresponding patternings within different sensory modalities. Stern stresses how important this recasting or translating is for intersubjectivity. This is because in varying the sensory modality, attention is not focused solely on the external behaviour expressed but towards the internal referent, the inner feelings of the baby which have given rise to some expression. In responding to the *feel* of this inner experience, the mother is echoing the feel rather than the form of expression *per se*.

Intensity, shape, time, motion and number

Daniel Stern identifies different elements within the repertoire of the infant's embodied flow of experiencing which can be picked up by others and shared.[6] These may include the *absolute intensity* of a movement; for example, babies may cry in a half-hearted or total fashion. There is also a shaping of intensity within the flow of energy. It could begin as intense and wind down, or go up and down. Babies may kick and move within a measured phrasing of time as well as different changes of beat. The whole sequence of communication will occur within a particular time span or duration. This will be matched by the mother's response. Finally, any movement will evoke a particular shape or form – it could be curving, up and down or expanding out and in. This again could be matched across different sensory modalities.

Such correspondence across sensory modalities begs the question of what is a consistent source within all? Stern suggests that these can include intensity, shape, time, motion and number. It appears that such qualities may be abstracted from any particular sensory modality and then recast. For example, we can translate an experience of smooth texture into sound, vision, taste and smell. We can translate a wavy shape into a sound, touch, taste and possibly smell too. Geschwind argued that such correspondences are vital for language and for all metaphors.[7] Stern found that matching occurred most frequently first in relation to intensity, second in terms of temporal qualities and shape.[6] Stern suggests that intensity and temporal patterns may be the earliest qualities that the baby can represent modally and at the earliest developmental stages. It is clear that the baby is immersed in temporal and rhythmic experiences in terms of uterine sounds, for example, of sucking, of rocking and soothing touch from a very early stage. Allen Schore understands these rhythmically soothing patterns as being crucial elements within the affective regulatory aspects of caring that enable the infant to make transitions between states or stages of more intense distress and calmer states.[8] The mother gradually 'calms the baby down' by introducing different rhythms in communicating. However, if she does not initially match some of the intensity, the baby may tend to become even more distressed.

It appears that in signalling attunement initially, the capacity to match intensity is important. It could be surmised that intensity most closely resembles inner affective states and moods. As adults, we may seek to achieve a similar effect by choosing music to match a current state of feeling; for example, *Carmina Burana* or music from *Prodigy* appear to express a high degree of intensity compared with Satie's *Gymnopédie*. New Age music is often despised for not expressing any intensity at all – which might be consistent with states of consciousness that are less focused on inner states than more transpersonal ones.

Suzanne Langer's proposal is that all art and language is a way of expressing feeling.[9] Art captures an element of felt life. Therefore, it is not surprising that we are highly attuned to matching and corresponding with these felt inner states in others. In this sense, the metaphors of music and dance are the closest analogues to bodily experiences of energy and flow subtly altering in response to each movement – always against a less variable or more invariant homoeostasis of rhythm and form against which each momentary alteration is mapped.

The difference between attunement and empathy

Empathy or *einfuehlung* was a term mainly connected with aesthetics.[10] It seemed to reflect the ideas involved in physiognomic perception later coined by Werner and Kaplan.[11] It involved an immersion into the experiential qualities of music or art so that the movement qualities could be discerned. In this sense, the term *empathy* originally seems to have connoted something more similar to attunement. Titchener described how we naturally feel ourselves into perceptual or imaginal experience in nature and art. Carl Rogers developed his approach to empathy over time.[12] In 1959, Rogers described empathy as a state which could be experienced without falling into over-identification but he also proposed that empathic understanding is a dialogic process in which the counsellor checks his understanding with the client for verification. In 1980, Rogers' account of empathy appears to have further developed from his experience and from the influence of

Gendlin. Empathy is described as a process of entering the other's world and 'becoming thoroughly at home in it'; 'it involves being sensitive moment by moment to the changing felt meanings . . . sensing meanings of which he or she is scarcely aware'.[12] This account of empathy appears to suggest a deeper immersion into the experiential world of the other not only within the flowing inner feelings but also towards their felt meaning. It is this emphasis on meaning that clarifies again the distinction between empathy and attunement.

For Stern the difference between attunement and empathy is that attunement is less cognitively based than empathy.[6] Empathy would involve a real immersion into the inner world of the infant and an effort to interpret or understand this inner state through concepts. Attunement may be an important step towards empathy but it does not need interpretation or words. The mother may speak to the baby but it is the tone and phrasing that is signalled rather than the words themselves. Attuning appears far more oriented towards creating and facilitating intersubjectivity; it appears to provide the very stuff of relationship. What else can be transacted between two persons other than something of themselves and their experiencing? By matching and playing with the baby's communications, the mother is signalling a willingness to join in something together with the baby. She does not have any overt purpose or aim other than enabling a joining of persons in a shared activity that can be communicated between them. Without the barrier of language, successful attunement seems to be experienced as something that allows the baby's flow to continue without hindrance. Stern noted how any slight misattunement appeared to stop the baby mid-track, whereas successful attunement did not appear to make any difference. The baby just continued along. However, it is also clear that attunement facilitates some effect on the baby's mood which may be enhanced and become more aroused with the mother's response. It is this aspect that is very interesting in that attunement appears to allow a new sense of self with other to be gradually formed. If the baby rises to a pitch of excitement and then appears to falter, the attuned mother will pick up the subtle shift and adjust so that the baby can wind down a little with ease. The mother responds directly and bodily to the flow of feeling, its intensity and direction rather than interpreting its meaning. If someone wants to join in a dance with others, they only have to follow and participate to be part of the whole group.

In this sense, empathy may use attuning capacities to feel such qualities and phrasing within the narrative flow of clients, within language and tonalities used in the telling. The bodily sensed experiencing of the world which begins in infant communication remains accessible throughout adult life, often most obviously in the field of the arts and poetry. Stern called this aspect of self the emergent aspect, the part of self that is operating at the basis of perception and experience prior to conceptualization and language.

Attunement within the therapeutic process

With the therapeutic process, a very different quality of contact can occur when a therapist or client centres their attention intentionally from the heart centre. It may allow a different experience of the client, a different kind of information may be there, a softer feeling about them may arise. It is a kind of mutual compassion in which the counsellor may feel more acceptance of him- or herself also.

At the same time, these processes occur to us anyway, very often out of consciousness. We are working with attuning to others in a series of nonverbal bodily communications. These can be observed micro-second by micro-second in filmed human communication. What is observable are the ways that each partner subtly echoes or responds nonverbally all the time to the other person – like a secret dance. We tend to act as if this is not happening, when it is the very stuff of happening between any two people. We can notice immediately at a glance how well two people are communicating or relating or getting on by observing the level of synchrony in movement, the matching of rhythm and intensity and absorption in the other's attention.

In meeting a person for the first time, we have to notice the relative level of intensity or mood they are conveying. Meeting a depressed, flat person with undue enthusiasm would not facilitate contact. Similarly, being depressed when meeting a very animated, excited person at a party would be perceived as flattening and perhaps negative. Although as therapists and counsellors we may not exactly match the other's intensity, we may show even by the way we slow down or change our tone of voice at particular moments that we are recognizing the low state in the other.

A more obvious kind of attunement may be perceived in comparing temporal beat and duration between therapist and client. Over time, it becomes more apparent to all therapists that a rhythmic pattern of dialogue or silence becomes acquired with each client within certain variations. In this temporal pulsing of responsivity between therapist and client, a great deal of attunement is conveyed as well as a kind of stable beat to sustain the fluctuations. Often in the moments between words, it is as if a kind of invisible echo continues to resonate both in the therapist and client. A deeper sound from the words continues to affect both at an experiential level. The silence is almost like a time of bodily assimilation and absorption; but in the context of attunement it is like an attuning process going on. The therapist's response represents the degree to which he or she is fitting with the communication of the client, or matching or recasting it to resonate with other related or deeper issues. It is possible for the therapist to attune in such a way that a more profound resonance and fit is sounded within the client. This again may be experienced in both therapist and client as a new sound, a new chord that has been created between them.

The capacity of the therapist to draw on what can be called a felt sense or a heart perception allows a drawing together of divergent strands – tones, colours within the communications of the other – for one quality to be known or understood. This kind of understanding is not one that translates neatly into any one concept or word, but it appears to allow a base for communication.

However, the intersubjective process and the intrasubjective process are both characterized by flux and change. In this sense, the active component of attuning to the other requires a capacity to follow movement without resisting. If we are listening to a piece of music, we lose it precisely at the moment when we start commenting on it to another person. In this sense, attuning is like diving into water and swimming along with the other person; we do not know where we are going. However, if we follow them we come upon the places where the other person stops and is unable to move or gets stuck in circles. When we recognize that what moves the flow is the synthesis of feeling and learning replayed in a new context of therapy, then it becomes clearer how the capacity to attune with clients is experienced as a primary sense of being connected with and understood – not necessarily in conceptual terms, but in a sense of mutuality or willingness to accompany someone.

Clients appear to be highly attuned to the nuances of therapists' communications also. In her research with clients reporting on the experience of being listened to, one client noted how it was evident when her therapist was not listening. Despite apparently making eye contact, the client noticed that the therapist became 'glazed'. This may be a shorthand way of noticing when the rhythm of attunement has become unmatched. As Stern reported on the baby who stopped and looked up at his mother when she responded less intensely to his communications, each of us has developed micro-acuity in reading responsiveness to others in movement matching – which is another way of describing attunement.

Facilitating attunement

Attunement requires a sounding-board and a way of adjustment. In the spiritual understanding of the heart centre, both of these are characteristic of the heart. Sometimes part of this attunement has been called 'aligning the heart'. The Sufic idea is that the heart can turn and respond to any aspect of living. If we attentionally align it or orientate it towards others, it appears to facilitate both contact and attentiveness and receptivity to others. For many years I learned this as a simple, almost unconscious technique which helped me to overcome resistance and a sense of being closed when I was about to embark on teaching or working with groups. At evening sessions, I often felt particular resistance to turning out and putting energy into a process. I learned that by having the idea of aligning my heart, imagining that my heart was focused entirely towards the people coming to the group, the resistance went. The resistance was often connected with negative and anxious thoughts. When my attention was focused on the heart centre, the thoughts became more background. In the foreground was simply a softer, more open and compassionate feeling in my heart. I was more conscious of the people coming to the class or group than of my resistance. I felt more human connection with the feelings and hopes which they brought to the group. It is something I continue to practise every day in my life – but it has become so habitual that I have almost forgotten the intentional process behind it.

Attunement requires a specificity of attention, more narrowly-focused on the deeper movement qualities that are being conveyed viscerally through fluctuations in intensity, temporal beat and duration. It is in the smaller shifts among these that we pick up discontinuities, fractures, uncertainties, gaps, conflicts, blocks and changes in flow. So we focus attention on the other and the echoing resonance within us at the same time. If you are less familiar in referring to your heart, you can just begin by noticing where your heart beats, where you feel your heart to be in your chest. Then imagine that you are gathering all your sense of self, of your mind and thoughts within your chest or heart area rather than your head. You may be aware of physical sensations in your chest. You can try imagining that there are perceptual systems operating from your heart or chest – so that you can see with your heart, or hear with your heart, or feel with your heart. Now try to pay attention to another person from your heart-centred perception.

It is worth experimenting with this if you are travelling on a bus or tube. First explore your perception and thoughts about your fellow passengers. You may notice clear distinctions that you are making about them, there may be ways of categorizing them, making assumptions about them, deciding that you like one person and not another. Now try switching into heart perception mode. When I try this, something quite dramatic happens. Instead of categorizing and separating from everyone, I feel an immediate sense of connection and kinship at an inner level, a more inclusive and less excluding way.

However, for many people, initially they may not be able to feel anything in the heart or chest area. It is a much vaguer, less tangible kind of knowing that can easily become lost within the louder clamour of continual thought processes. It is the same area that Gendlin's focusing works in when a person attempting to focus allows a vague, unclear, overall feeling about a situation to occur which may then be put into some kind of language or form of representation. It is primarily a bodily referent. It takes time to learn to attend to the heart and to the way we notice the other's effect on us through the heart. Needless to say, as within all therapeutic endeavour, the perception of heart can get distorted by our own preoccupations and obsessions which we may project on to others. This is why there is some emphasis on purification of the heart within spiritual practices.

Attunement, like any meditative practice, requires a capacity to let go. Putting aside our current preoccupations, or bracketing assumptions, does not perhaps capture the sense of needing to actively drop thoughts, or to fall into a more open space where our attention is mainly focused on following the other's process. Attunement as focus would require us to fade out all extraneous information in order to become absorbed in one aspect – a particular narrative, a particular feeling, a particular interrelational theme being played out between therapist and client at this moment. It has all the qualities of joining the dance, playing a game, improvisation and experiment entirely focused on interaction rather than on the inner process. It is like an absorption within a flow, yet it requires a kind of simultaneous play-back to notice the resonances within our experiencing too. From this perspective, the notion of attunement casts the role of therapist in a less cautious and inhibited light in which he or she may venture to offer a different interpretation each time.

Clients may experience therapists as highly attuned whether they speak or not, but what is challenging for all therapists to realize is that there is nowhere to hide in the therapeutic space. Their own engagement will be entirely evident in the experience of attunement from their clients. It requires a capacity to focus attention on the other's movement, a capacity to let go and surrender to the present moment, and a capacity to feel the resonance that is received in return from this focused attention.

Some exercises to explore attunement

1. Listen to a particular piece of music and translate it into movement or an image or images.
2. Similarly, try looking at a picture and imagining it as a particular kind and style of music.
3. There is a Buddhist practice called *kasina*. Focus on something such as a plant, intensely and with deep appreciation. Then turn away. An emptiness is left in the mind denoting the absence of the plant. Then a mood or gesture, a kind of after-image of the plant, begins to surface within the inner attention. This may be repeated so that it strengthens each time. The idea is that what one sees is the gesture, the inner quality, of that particular plant or focus – a kind of felt essence[13] (p. 227).
4. Consider the overall ambience of a social gathering and pinpoint the main quality or tone that is least variable among the flux.

5. In any human situation, try observing from a mental, naming or categorizing perspective, and then try observing and feeling from your heart.
6. Observe how you make transitions to adjust to different situations, home, travel, work, friends. Alternatively, notice what happens to assist you to move from one client to another. What is it that is going on to enable you to do this?

Moving beyond attunement

Within the therapeutic process, or in any human encounter, once we have established contact, we need also to make a kind of receptive or invitational presence to allow more communication to unfold. In the context of a heart-based modality of listening, I call this *amplification*.

6 | Amplification: A Relational Sense of Spaciousness

ARTHUR DEIKMAN makes a simple distinction between different kinds of consciousness in relation to meditation.[1] The first is the usual, everyday kind of doing mode which he terms *instrumental*. It involves action, clear definitions in perception, objects and lines of causality. The best example is driving a car in busy traffic. The second is called *receptive consciousness*. The best example he gives is soaking in a hot bath. By contrast, this kind of consciousness or attention is receptive, undifferentiated, more about process, diffused boundaries and background feeling. To try this out, he suggests looking at a partner's face or a tree or flower. First, look at it with an analytical attention. Then look only receptively, being open to whatever emerges into awareness. He reports how most people find this yields a sense of more depth, meaning or even mystery to the encounter. He attributes some of the shift to a move towards a different, less self-centred focus, more resonant with environment.

Jung used the term *amplification* as a way of extending and elaborating on the archetypal aspects of his patients' symbolic material.[2] In the context of sound, musical instruments and amplifiers extend sound, making it louder. When we amplify a gesture we increase its scope and dimensions. Within therapy, we amplify the communications of clients in different ways.

One way of amplifying is akin to the philosophy of Taoism. We allow flow. We make space for, are receptive to, open towards what is simply happening without interference. For example, silence can provide this kind of amplification. The client's words keep echoing and resonating in the space between therapist and client. Amplifying is subtly different from the adoption of a mindful attitude, or cultivation of spaciousness and openness *per se*. Amplifying provides the metaphor of a vessel which can allow expansion and resonance. It is a paradox both containing and infinite. One of the most extraordinary aspects of therapeutic process is how making space for something to exist, to be acknowledged, to be allowed or included is healing in itself. The sense of allowing space is a sense of holding. It has a generosity and a compassion that is different from just neutrality or empty space. Not doing, allowing flow is enough.

> To talk little is natural
> High winds do not last all morning.
> Heavy rain does not last all day.

and . . .

> That which shrinks
> must first expand.
> That which fails
> Must first be strong.
> That which is cast down
> Must first be raised.
> Before receiving
> There must be giving.

Here, relationally, the attitude of spaciousness creates an allowing kind of environment. Such allowing appears friendly, inviting, warm, because it is an intention held by the therapist towards the client. The intention is one where the therapist is trying not to impede or intrude on to the other. At the same time, the therapist's presence is perceived by the other as available, as fluid, as alive.

AMPLIFICATION

Beyond the allowing of flow there can be another kind of amplification. This magnifies the original sound or communication. In the same way that a mother reflects back the baby's smile in a wider face or with a sound and gesture, the therapist can extend the message. This can be in intensifying the affective or symbolic content as if adding more charge or meaning to the communication. It can be by emphasizing the situational or contextual framework to what has been said.

A third way whereby we can amplify clients' communications is to simply follow the flow of the narrative or meaning and invite further exploration. The topic is opened up by reflection or questions or by following the flow of the symbolic content in dreams and metaphors. A fourth way in which amplification may be used is to play with or create something new with what has been said. This is like Winnicott's notion of the transitional object.[4] The therapist engages with what is being communicated with some sense of aliveness, allowing something to emerge further from exploration.

From the perspective of the client, the observation of the therapist's attention may be experienced entirely differently. In the therapist's capacity to attend, the client will experience a level of being heard. It is as if attention is like a radio aerial which can pick up different patterns of information. When the therapist is open to picking up more information, it appears that clients are sensitive to this. They experience it as a kind of spatial, allowing process which enables them to relax and unfold a little more.

Amplifying as a kind of yielding environment

It is as if the therapist is providing an environment with hard or soft furniture, yielding or unyielding surfaces, textures of different kinds of smoothness and resonance. As a kind of amplifier, the therapist's attention allows different degrees of amplification for the communication of the client to echo and resound. When a client says something and the therapist engages without this quality of allowing spatiality or amplification, the client feels more restricted and hemmed in by the thoughts and words of the therapist. Their pressure perhaps intrudes upon the client. Therapists may indicate this kind of amplification in different ways: it could be through silence, or through echoing the direction of flow of the client.

Sometimes the therapist's attention can withdraw from the client and go somewhere else. This may well be perceived as cold, unresponsive and perhaps even deadening. What is suggested in this is that attention is not something automatic and mechanical like a light beam. It involves an actual style of embodiment and orientation which is picked up by the client as a series of many movements and adjustments as the therapist follows the process and movement of the client. It is by definition a dynamic and fluid series of intentions towards allowing the client to keep moving and unfolding within a series of dimensions.

Perhaps the client experiences this kind of spacious and accompanying attention as another kind of vitality contour. The vitality contour is shaped by the adjustments between therapist and client, and while there is a chronological sequence of shifting flux and transitions, the invariant factor is of a kind of steady accompanying mutual awareness and responsiveness. It is as if the client is held within another beam of response which can be steady throughout the changes. This then corresponds with the way we use the term *holding*. It could be related to the infant child experience in the way the mother has to continually adjust her arms and body to the movements of the child. The child's experience could be of one continuous environment that adapts and moulds itself to its movements. The paradox is how the experience of expansion and spaciousness and allowance can be felt as holding and containing. It has to be explained within the mutual embodiment of such experience. Spaciousness is experienced as room to move around in. Emptiness does not have that possibility of movement; it seems to imply a need to cling to something very minimal or that is disappearing into a large void.

Amplification and environmental affordance

In Gibson's approach to perception, outlined in Chapter 2, it was noted that perceptual systems have evolved to assist an organism's navigation or orientation in an environment.[5] Gibson stressed that *we do not live in space, we live in places*. Perception is thus a meeting place of adaptation between person and environment in which the environment is perceived as offering differing affordances or possibilities for the survival of the organism.

Applying these ideas within the therapeutic process, the qualities of spaciousness and breadth of attention will offer affordances from the different aspects of texture and flow according to many simultaneous perceptual modalities and experiences which are being responded to within the narratives of the session, its relation to other sessions, the environment of the room, access to the room, the context of the day, the place, work and the world situation. Each therapeutic session can be evoked as a trajectory through spatial and textural qualities which contain affective and conative elements. Space is then primarily experienced as place or orientation. In the presence of the therapist, and in the place of therapy, the client will experience the evenly focused attention as a wide field of possibility in which there can be response and meeting. The invariance of attention is in the evenly accommodating attention to whatever arises, a lighter and less focused quality which succeeds by reducing responsiveness to one element while allowing a quality of response to everything that happens. It is like a smoothing out of tension between conflicting issues because there is no undulation or undue stress on any one thing. It is like a very even, sustained rhythm which does not alter whatever tune is played. The rhythm sustains the tune and keeps the music going without directing it into any particular place. It is like a steady rhythm of heartbeat.

Example of amplifying attention within a therapy session

A psychotherapist reported on the effect of meditation prior to a session with a client.[6] She described how she adopted a Buddhist meditation where she imagined watching a log flow downstream until it disappeared out of sight.

> By this practice, I become unaware of the linear time flow. I find it quite enjoyable to become the observer of the free associated images and feelings....

She went on to describe how her client is usually very anxious and nervous, unable to control her anger and the ceaseless activity of her mind. On this day, it seemed as though the client entered the room differently; she looked around the walls and then sat in her chair making an exhalation as she sat down. She had the feeling that she was looking around to see 'the feeling of energy in the room'. She reported how after a few moments' silence, as she started talking, she felt more in attunement with herself. Her body gestures were more freely and harmoniously flowing rather than previous more erratic fragments of thoughts and feelings. The client reported that she had a vaguely 'good' feeling that involved a large sense of peace and calm in her chest.

> When I invited her to describe to me the way she indicated a feeling that was subtle, elusive, hard to describe and more than can be put into words.... For example, as the client was becoming aware of the vague feeling of calmness and peace she got in touch with a serene state of mind that is normally overwhelmed by anxious thoughts and charged emotionally with anger. In these few moments of calmness, the client received a new, explicit meaning or understanding of 'accepting another person's differences'. The client after a moment of silence said in surprise:

'I think I can understand now how difficult it must be for other people to connect with me because I am so nervous all the time and full of anger. I am so much in my story and therefore not giving others the opportunity to connect with me.'

This account offers a powerful example of the way that the capacity to find a spacious even kind of attention and presence can allow the client to move in a bigger space within his or her own world.

Amplifying attention as a rhythm of space

The consistent pulse of attention creates a rhythm that supports activity and change. In Sufic philosophy and culture, architecture and music represent rhythmic patterns linking spaces harmoniously, combining both serial and circular symmetrical patterns.

Bakhtiar suggests that:

> The role of time in traditional architecture lies in rhythm, the succession of boundary lines that allow an unbroken rhythmic flow, like the waves of the sea; macrocosmically and microcosmically, nature has disposed itself in rhythm. Only through rhythm is one able to escape the prison of time. Nature contains continual repetition, inspiring man to imitate her in her mode of operation through an open-ended continuous movement system. The many curves and arabesques within Islamic art are expressing the continual flux of creation, of expansion and contraction, ascendance and descendance. This flow of form is a continuous transformation of space and possibility. (p. 87)[7]

In the same way, the source of our attention and consciousness allows for continual new moments of awareness to come into being and others to fade away. Attention is a creative summoning into being of possibilities and so it is experienced spatially as places to move in or inhabit. Free attention provides a kind of mirror-like space which is open. When we direct our attention towards another person they feel our attention rest on them. Sheldrake suggests that attention is a projection of the mind.[8]

Mystics have perceived the heart as offering infinite spaciousness. As the basis of consciousness as feeling, it presents an infinite capacity to pick up, to attend to and to care for others. One of the roots of the word *tolerance* comes from the notion of allowing space for the other to exist.

Amplifying attention

How can we amplify attention in the heart?

As with meditational practices which emphasize bare attention, mindfulness or with a phenomenological attitude of applying equal attention to all aspects of perception, this mode of attention is a broad and open kind. However, I wish to emphasize a less visually oriented way of describing this. If we were to consider such an openness to what appears as a felt and heard manifestation, then the spaciousness has a quality of being received, and held within attention as hearing and feeling space.

Amplification is a quality of presence in which the echoes of what is said can fully resound in the space and time that is needed. I am stressing metaphors of sound and feeling to create a more personal and contactful quality within the spaciousness of attention. This provides a profound sense of being received, whether that is experienced in the subliminal awareness of breathing and embodied presence within silence or whether it is perceived within an open and inviting verbal response which encourages further expansion and exploration in the flow of what is being expressed. Essentially, amplification is an allowance of flow. It is like water falling on to a surface which can spread as far as it needs. The interesting aspect of this allowing of flow is how relaxing it is for the receiver. Even in an individual way this can work. For example, a fast and effective way to facilitate relaxation is to sit in a meditational kind of posture and close the eyes. By simply paying attention to whatever arises in awareness and following it with attention, a progressive and deep state of relaxation is reached within a few minutes.

Amplifying is the same kind of attention applied to the other. Going with the flow. In focusing, one of the most powerful aspects of its effects is how, simply by allowing room for some aspect of experience to exist or to have a place, a shift can occur. In many ways, perhaps this is an aspect of therapeutic process that is worthy of further investigation. How it is that by consciously attending to something, and intentionally allowing more place or space in awareness for this thing to coexist with other aspects of experiencing, a significant shift in relation to self and others can occur such as Gendlin describes in *Focusing*.[9] Even more interesting is how, after two days of intensive work with focusing, I found the quality of my attunement and listening to clients extraordinarily and subtly altered to a much deeper level of contact.

Exercises for amplifying attention

1. Try closing your eyes and simply paying attention to any sensation or image that arises. Just follow each one with your attention for as long as it needs. This exercise promotes a deep sense of relaxation very quickly.
2. Sit with your current awareness of being without doing anything with it at all. Deliberately let go of all injunctions and agendas.
3. Lying on the floor, notice if and how your body wants to move, and follow the movement as long as it needs to take.
4. When listening to your clients, notice what is most foregrounded in their communications and allow something to expand or deepen as much as it needs, either through

silence, through encouraging exploration or intensification of the theme.
5. Cultivate a continuously yielding and allowing attitude to whatever feelings are occurring within the heart centre as you listen to clients without resisting.

7 | Going Deeper: Reverberation and Depth

THE THIRD MODALITY OF HEART or relational listening may be related to Buber's 'I and thou' mode of meeting another person: 'The primary word I-Thou can be spoken only with the whole being' (p. 24).[1] It is a fundamental capacity to meet and to be open and to contact an eternal kind of reverberation between myself and another in relation. Having moved through attunement to the other, and an allowing of the other, in depth I allow myself to be moved by and to reverberate with the other in a profound sense of mutual relationship. It is the final point of meeting and resonance that stays with me after the meeting has finished.

David Michael Levin describes this profound quality of listening to the being of another as *hearkening*.[2] It is a kind of hearing without attachments which opens us to the field of sound itself. Silence is the ground from which sound emerges. According to the Lakotan culture there is no word for silence; only a word meaning the absence of noise. In our culture perhaps the word for noise will disappear as a fundamental given and there will only be a word for the absence of silence.

Within psychotherapy however, the sounds of silence are played out in many different keys and modulations. It becomes a living environment from which every spoken communication is more clearly outlined, like black forms on a white background. For example, very often at the beginning of a session, there are several minutes of silence which provide a significant context and ground for whatever follows. Silence at the end of a session has another quality of providing a softer way to make a transition between ending and exiting from the room. Within therapeutic dialogue silence paces, opens spaces, clarifies gaps and non-meetings. It also allows words and meanings to amplify further and to reverberate not only in the therapeutic hour, but perhaps in succeeding weeks, months, even years.

Beyond the awareness of attunement and the receptivity of amplification, the capacity to reverberate with another's communication requires a capacity to sense the relation between sound and silence, or figure and ground. It is the context between the two that designates meaning within Gestalt psychology. This kind of listening occurs at rare and unexpected moments. Something is said, and it seems to strike a chord which goes on reverberating profoundly, or poignantly. In Gestalt psychotherapy, the deeper the awareness of the ground, the more meaning will arise from the relation of figure to ground. If we are alone on a high mountain on a starry night, gazing out at the universe at a significant moment of life change, then any event or experience that occurs in such a context is likely to have enormous meaning. The context of place is vast and deep, the context of human life is dwarfed by the enormities of the universe and time and space, and our own small part of the story is cast in relation to this.

Strangely enough, having written this piece I came across precisely such an account by the anonymous Zapatista non-leader of the new style of revolutionary tactics.[3] He describes his first journey up a mountain towards what would be the beginning of an enormous long struggle. Feeling overwhelmed with the physical exertion and loneliness, he looked up at the sky:

> I saw a sky that was a gift and a relief – no more like a promise ... I stayed looking knowing that I'd have to climb up that wretched hill to see this dawn ... knowing that all of that – and much more would come later – is what had made it possible for that moon, those stars, and the Milky Way to be there and no other place.

As he watches, a star falls, and he says to himself: '"That's what we are, fallen stars that barely scratch the sky of history with a scrawl" and this symbolised the thirty year struggle that unfolded to open a crack in history.'

In rare moments within the context of therapy, human encounter and in meditation, we can feel a similar profundity of meaning that has the same night-sky kind of vastness. It may occur when a client brings a dream or an experience which has been of great and healing significance. Sometimes, a new reconciliation or contact between estranged family members after many years occurs in a constructive way during the therapeutic process. Sometimes, when therapy comes to an end, there is a sense of similar relation to a far bigger scheme of things that has been witnessed during the time together.

A core sense of reverberation also occurs when the experience of the client is profoundly shocking to our sense of human existence. A client who had been brought up in a religious institution from the age of 2 told me that she had been known only by a number and was only told her name when she left at 14. Such a communication ruptures many cherished ideas about human life, and the ground on which the therapy is taking place is rocked. Such a sense of the earth quaking echoes the impact that one person can have on another – shaking and quaking their sense of being – literally a profound and core impact.

In a different context, I met with a good friend who had been working for an international agency in a brutal conflict. During our conversation, he recounted a particularly traumatic experience of rescuing young children who had been forgotten after their dead mother had been found. As he recounted this to me, I realized I had read this same story in a newspaper. The story suddenly shifted from an I–it mode of a daily journalistic news-story to one in which I felt in profound encounter with the same events through my relation with this friend. Again, in this reverberation of meaning that expands through different levels of existence and context, something seems to resound like a gong, creating deeper and deeper spaces, and echoes are called up within us. It does not have to arise from such existential shocks alone; we can find that these depths of reverberation occur with intensities of feeling, in response to art or any human situation. Such situations were termed *archetypal* by Jung, and their main characteristic was their affective and sometimes numinous effect on depth.

In spiritual practices, or recorded mystical experiences, affective experiences can be of such an intensity that the participant feels almost overwhelmed. It is as if the capacities to feel feeling itself are stretched. It is these kinds of experiences which may have a life-changing effect on the participant. Jung described them as a direct gnosis of the numinosum which is a value that we all seek to find. Once it is felt within, it cannot be corrupted or taken away.

One of the qualities of these brief, striking moments of reverberation is that their meaning cannot be distilled. The reverberation appears to go on opening up questions and previous certainties to something deeper than what is known or understood. It is this sense of depth that is linked with our sense of meaning; in these moments the line between life and death seems clearer and held within the mystery of the cosmos.

Intentional use of holding figure/ground

As an exercise, within workshops, an intentional application of this kind of mode of attending has been tried. The suggestion was to imagine the background behind the person and to simultaneously hold that person and their communications in relation to this background. When some participants tried this, they appeared to find that there was more immediate access to knowing directly or intuitively what the client was saying. A rich, accompanying flow of images appeared to emerge which were highly accurate and attuned to the communications of the client.

Another way of approaching this kind of awareness intentionally would be to combine both previous perspectives. In other words, the task would be to hold in concurrent awareness the sense of the sound of the person in relation to a wider ground of possibility and openness. It is as if the present relationship is received also in relation to a wider field of possibilities as if wave and particle are included. This seems to evoke what Buber described as *inclusion of the other*.[1]

For the listener to focus on the deeper ground, this requires a capacity to let go of current preoccupations towards an openness, whether this is perceived spatially or acoustically or as heart-based attention – as an openness towards consciousness as feeling what is present. In focusing, Gendlin found early on that the focusing process was considerably altered by the kind of preparation of inner space that could be achieved.[4] At this level of listening, the different degrees to which a therapist may be accustomed to enter deeper states of consciousness from meditational practice will make a difference to the quality of reverberation that can be felt and held. The sense of being rocked or shaken or stirred by another is illustrative of the depths of being to which we can be moved by experience.

The word *depth* has a physiognomic similarity to faith. To me, both sound like a foot moving through soft earth and landing deep down. Depth allows a greater drop before landing. There is a sense of something being moved through, an open space, an unknown, hidden place like a cave or walking on freshly dug earth on a dark night, when nothing can be seen. There is only the felt sense of familiar body movement and the trust in one's feet to lift up from the ground and to find a new place on the ground to go forward. I think this is akin to the experience of deepening. Something is hollowed out and something is touched that feels more and more fundamental and core.

From this perspective, this third aspect of heart listening is one which depends on the attitude and values of the practitioner. The intensity and depth of these rare experiences of hearkening to another or reverberating can easily be avoided and often are. They may threaten both therapist and client with a quality of relationship and meaning for which they are not prepared.

Exercises relevant to deepening and reverberation

I cannot offer any simple exercise as it would be too trite. Instead, I suggest two areas for contemplation and enquiry.

1. How is it that depth is felt to be satisfying to us and how is it that surface experiences are intrinsically unsatisfying?
2. What is it that deepens my capacity to feel depth?

Attunement, amplification and depth

These three unfolding ways of resonating with others are in fact one seamless capacity to feel with another in a profound and heartfelt way. They can be compared with the sacred Sanskrit word/sound for the divine ground of being – A–U–M. They represent a willingness to open and begin relating to another person, a receptivity to open and share further to understand, and a capacity to be stirred, moved and affected profoundly by humanness and life itself. In fact, to bring this down to earth, these three modalities of listening occur many times every day with family, friends and colleagues and work situations in different phrasings and patterns, at varying levels of intensity. If we observe, we may notice how these arcs or vitality contours of attunement, amplification and reverberation are repeated.

Here is a very silly example. I encounter my son on the sofa early one evening. My attuned sense of his state is of a sense of something flattened and a bit glum. He says, 'Buffy is not on.' I look at the television screen, and to add insult to injury they are showing a programme of a game of snooker. My voice responds with prosody – making a sound that reflects sympathy and also slight exaggeration. He responds: 'It's not like Thursdays at all.' I laugh with him about the snooker adding insult to injury. By this time our contact has moved from attunement to the flat feeling of being disappointed and having had a mediocre kind of day, to being amused at the feelings television programmes induce in us; we are in a kind of joking synchrony. The interaction finishes. This is a kind of 'cheering up' vitality contour I have played out with him. It probably echoes numerous similar phrases of contact we have enjoyed since his infancy. The feeling we end with is sort of comforting – to me because I feel I have connected with him and experience some kind of closeness through the attunement to his flatness and the slight sense of absurdity into laughter. For him, I do not know, but I feel it is some kind of energizing effect from the moment of shared human contact in a depressed state, like the toddler who is playing alone and then crawls towards his mother for a moment or two before manifesting more purpose and energy into his play.

When I live more from my heart as a centre of awareness, I find that I am naturally more in tune with others and have far more inner space in which to receive and welcome them. I do not have any way of accounting for this, but I rely on it to assist me in every human encounter.

Conclusion

I HAVE TRACED some of the ways in which we are already attuned to the most subtle and intricate of relational processes and understandings. I have suggested that a sensibility that is based on heart and feeling is one which includes rationality and emotion and in a way goes beyond both as an integrating ground of knowing awareness. This approach to the heart as a centre of feeling and knowing is stressed both from mystical traditions and now intriguingly with some potential scientific support. What happens if we attend to others from a conscious heart-focused intention? It appears that we have access to a more connected field of understanding which permits an allowing space in which to meet and feel in touch.

Psychotherapy is far from a magical cure. Who can claim to know what essentially helps people? At a simple level, I would suggest two key positive ingredients. One is that therapy can assist a person to be in relation to themselves in a more comfortable, supportive and empowering way – such that, in a sense, they befriend themselves more. The second is that therapy can assist someone to relate better to others and therefore to feel more connected with life. Both arise from thousands of tiny moments of attunement and attempts to understand which may assist a different sense of self with others to come into being.

At present, scientific paradigms are being challenged in relation to consciousness and attention. The extensive, painstaking and creative work of Rupert Sheldrake has endeavoured to point to the non-locality of the mind and the way we are sensitive to the attention of others either through staring, or even if someone stares at a photo.[1] His staring experiments have been conducted with a high number of participants, and the findings show that this is a phenomenon which is real, even if we cannot explain it. Psychotherapy has described the significance of thinking about clients or being preoccupied by them in absence for many years without being too concerned with a scientific paradigm to support these startling informal assertions about the role of attention.

Attention is a phenomenon that appears to have a number of effects which are like environmental affordances. It can provide a holding, it can provide a kind of spaciousness, it can provide a kind of close contact, it can provide a sense of confirmation. In all these ways, attention can offer a place or a sense of being and relatedness. It appears that clients are sensitive to the qualities of attention offered by therapists. Much of the effort in working as therapists arises from the work involved in creating sustained and available attention to others.

One of the central problems facing us in an overcrowded world of diminishing resources is our capacity to be open to or attentive to strangers and migrants. The usual response is one that comes from a 'top–down', categorizing and judgemental perspective and that reinforces fears and prejudices. Primitive responses of threat prevent us from any kind of feeling response that might come from the heart. This is an area that psychotherapy does not address but is one that challenges us all and will increasingly do so.

Recently, I was waiting to board a plane. It had been delayed. All of us stood at the threshold of the plane for about ten minutes. What was holding us up was a small group of people from a very different culture. They did not speak English. They had discovered they were all separated on the flight and were demanding to be able to sit together as a group. Even in this tiny, unimportant moment of waiting, I watched myself go through some impatience, irritation and negative thoughts and reactions as the crew attempted to accommodate their needs. But then, by focusing my attention towards them from my heart, there was a palpable shift of reaction. From a 'bottom–up' perspective, immediately, I felt closer to them, more accepting of their sense of vulnerability and strangeness in a foreign land and a need to be together. I felt the impatience slip away. I felt a kind of respect for their being different without having to fit into 'normal' ways of boarding a plane. It is a very small example, but in the current climate of increasing so-called syndromes of rage, it is worthwhile pointing out that there are different ways of perceiving that are available to all of us, and we have this in our heart centre.

The profession of psychotherapy is now resting on a hundred years of intensive and sincere effort to glean complex and valuable insights into the nature of the psyche, but it is important to recognize that theory can only facilitate our ways of understanding and feeling more for the client. Theory will help us to know about rather than know the client. Such knowing rests on the shifting ground of sentience and experiencing – as forms of feeling.

This book has attempted to bring together two different worlds, one derived from thousands of years of spiritual aspirations and disciplined focus, the other from contemporary disciplines that are more focused on the implicit and experiential base of cognition and intersubjectivity. The linking point is the heart as a potent symbol of the human capacity for love and for altruism. If we are informed primarily through sentience and feeling and not merely through hard-wired intelligence it may be our one source of hope. It is also why it is so hard because it means we have to face pain and suffering. Much of the time we do not want to feel, and our culture attempts to provide more and more ways to avoid this.

As a final note, I include an account of an experience from meditation. I think it speaks to all of this.

An inner feeling vision

I felt as though within the warmth of this darkness. I was aware of going within and down into depths. I was struck by the notion of warmth and coldness as different images from light and dark. So often we focus on these visual aspects. Metaphors of light are played to capture spirituality, and darkness signals shadow, something excluded from the light. But then we can get caught into the externals of vision, we look outwards towards the sun, we look out into the cosmos. Such notions of spiritual evolution can suggest that we journey out into space, moving outwards into the dark, void-like space as we go towards the sun. This is daunting, it feels cold, empty, distant, alien.

Yet when we contemplate warmth we are directly connected to something felt rather than seen. It is immediate, spontaneous, something that is within us, within our living flesh. In the meditation, I felt I was going within as if it were like going within the Earth. We forget so much that at the core of the Earth is a burning intense core of fire. We live on the concrete edges of our planet, entirely neglecting all those layers beneath and between the surface and the core. So this inner volcano-shaped anguish (I was feeling prior to the meditation) may be like those neglected, unattended rocky layers underneath everything.

I work often with others' depression and sadness. It has sometimes occurred to me that depression may be linked with a kind of neglect and inattention to our soul, to our inner depths and surfaces. These are the places of feeling. These are our sources of sensitivity and knowing, the place of heart. We cannot know the divine within us without feeling – not thinking, not seeing, but feeling. So perhaps it is no wonder that it is these deeper layers that are awakened and exposed as cleaning takes place. Like gems that are revealed within rocks, as sediments of thoughts and habits are removed, the crystalline tendrils of feeling are made available to us. It is only through infinitely refined feeling that we can perceive the field of the divine. It has often seemed that we have to stretch enormously within to bear the intensity of such glimpses.

So through feeling, bearing feeling, we can reach our core; and, for a moment, there was a feeling of being consumed by this central core. Luminous flames consumed my essence and were my essence – just like the sun. Then it suddenly came to me: the whole of this conception was the same as the one of Hell itself! And it was such a surprising and shocking thought that it is still hard to hold.

Could it be like this? We fear to feel. Feeling is painful. So we create a notion of Hell in which there are unbearable torments of feeling. In our fear, we numb and cut ourselves from our inner reality, our inner core, our source, our home, our hearth, our eternal flame, our own sun.

In the beginning, the Earth was a piece of the sun, spun out and cooling down to make our home.

In the beginning, we were one with divinity until denser and denser layers spun around our soul, and we were left to only focus on the outside, the edges of our selves.

The divine presence within our heart is neither heat nor light, but it is something to feel directly.

In the end, it is from this tiniest, subtlest feeling that all which is at the core of the universe can be known from within, and manifested humanly through heart to others.

It is just that we have to dare to feel, bear to feel, and to be consumed by love.

Much gratitude is due to the researchers and thinkers who have contributed new ways of describing the small, apparently insignificant moments of human relationship and of our sense of self. Fundamentally, the naming of such experiencing and relational art can only substantiate human worth and values in a corporate, market-driven world.

The only lasting beauty is the beauty of the heart – Rumi

Notes

1 Lawrence, D. H. (1980) From 'Know Deeply', in *The Complete Poems*, Penguin Books, London, p. 427.

Preface

1 See www.srcm.org

Introduction

1 Gendlin, E. (1978) *Focusing*. Bantam Books, New York.
2 Stern, D. (1985) *The Interpersonal World of the Infant*. Basic Books, New York.
3 Stern, D. *et al.* (1998) Non-interpretative mechanisms in psychoanalytic therapy: the 'something more' than interpretation. *International Journal of Psycho-Analysis* 79, pp. 903–921.
4 Stern, D. (1999) 'Vitality contours: the temporal contour of feelings as the basic unit for constructing the infant's social experience', in P. Rochat (ed.), *Early Social Cognition: Understanding Others in the First Months of Life*. Lawrence Erlbaum, New Jersey.
5 Trevarthen, C. and Hubley, P. (1978) 'Secondary intersubjectivity: confidence, confiders and acts of meaning in the first year', in A. Locke, *Action, Gesture and Symbol*. Academic Press, New York.

6 Trevarthen, C. (1994) 'The self born in intersubjectivity: the psychology of an infant communicating', in U. Neisser (ed.), *The Perceiving Self*. Cambridge University Press, Cambridge.
7 Gibson, J. J. (1978) *The Ecological Approach to Visual Perception*. Houghton Mifflin, Boston, MA.
8 Damasio, A. (1996) *Descartes' Error: Emotion, Reason and the Human Brain*. Papermac, London.
9 Damasio, A. (1999) *The Feeling of What Happens: Body and Emotion in the Making of Consciousness*. William Heinemann, London.
10 Epstein, M. (1997) *Thoughts Without a Thinker: Psychotherapy from a Buddhist Perspective*. Duckworth, London.
11 Welwood, J. (ed.) (1983) *Awakening the Heart: East/West Approaches to Psychotherapy and the Healing Relationship*. Shambhala, Boulder, CO.
12 Speeth, K. (1982) On psychotherapeutic attention. *Journal of Transpersonal Psychology*, pp. 141–159.
13 Coltart, N. (1992) *Slouching Towards Bethlehem: And Further Psychoanalytic Explorations*. Free Association Books, London.
14 Kornfield, J. (1994) *A Path with Heart: A Guide Through the Perils and Pitfalls of Spiritual Life*. Rider Books, London.
15 Brandon, D. (1983) 'Nowness in the helping relationship', in J. Welwood (ed.) *Awakening the Heart*. Shambhala, Boulder, CO.
16 Crook, J. and Fontana, D. (eds) (1990) *Space in Mind: East–West Psychology and Contemporary Buddhism*. Element Books, Dorset, UK.
17 Almaas, A. H. (1998) *Essence with the Elixir of Enlightenment*. Samuel Weiser Inc., York Beach, ME.

Chapter 1

1 Trevarthen, C. and Hubley, P. (1978) 'Secondary intersubjectivity: confidence, confiders and acts of meaning in the

first year', in A. Locke, *Action, Gesture and Symbol*. Academic Press, New York.

2 Varela, F., Thompson, E. and Rosch, E. (1993) *The Embodied Mind: Cognitive Science and Human Experience*. MIT Press, London.

3 Stolorow, R. (2000) From isolated minds to experiential worlds; an intersubjective space odyssey. *American Journal of Psychotherapy*, 54 (2), pp. 183–229.

4 Trevarthen, C. (1994) 'The self born in intersubjectivity: the psychology of an infant communicating', in U. Neisser (ed.) *The Perceiving Self*. Cambridge University Press, Cambridge.

5 Meltzoff, A. N. and Moore, M. K. (1977) Imitation of facial and manual gestures by human neonates. *Science*, 198, pp. 75–78.

6 Merleau-Ponty, M. (1962) *Phenomenology of Perception*, trans. C. Smith. Routledge & Kegan Paul, London.

7 Schore, A. (1996) *Affect Regulation and the Origins of Self: The Neurobiology of Emotional Development*. Lawrence Erlbaum, New Jersey.

8 Stern, D. (1985) *The Interpersonal World of the Infant*. Basic Books, New York.

9 Rochat, P. and Striano, T. (1999) 'Social-cognitive development in the first year', in P. Rochat (ed.) *Early Social Cognition: Understanding Others in the First Months of Life*. Lawrence Erlbaum, New Jersey.

10 Pipp, S. (1994) 'Infants' knowledge of self, other and relationship', in U. Neisser (ed.) *The Perceiving Self*. Cambridge University Press, Cambridge.

11 Stern, D. *et al.* (1998) Non-interpretative mechanisms in psychoanalytic therapy: the 'something more' than interpretation. *International Journal of Psycho-Analysis*, 79, pp. 903–921.

12 Stern, D. (1999) 'Vitality contours: the temporal contour of feelings as the basic unit for constructing the infant's social experience', in P. Rochat (ed.) *Early Social Cognition:*

Understanding Others in the First Months of Life. Lawrence Erlbaum, New Jersey.
13 Langer, S. (1979) *Mind: An Essay on Human Feeling,* Vol. 2. Johns Hopkins University Press, Boston, MA.
14 Myers, S. (2000) Empathic listening: reports on the experience of being heard. *Journal of Human Psychology,* 40 (2) spring, pp. 148–173.

Chapter 2

1 Vivekenanda, Swami (1973) *Raj Yoga: Patanjali's Yoga Aphorisms.* Advaita Ashram, Calcutta, India.
2 Rilke, R. M. (1989) *The Listening Self,* trans. D. M. Levin. Routledge, London.
3 Stern, D. *et al.* (1998) Non-interpretative mechanisms in psychoanalytic therapy: the 'something more' than interpretation. *International Journal of Psycho-Analysis,* 79, pp. 903–921.
4 Varela, F., Thompson, E., and Rosch, E. (1993) *The Embodied Mind: Cognitive Science and Human Experience.* MIT Press, London.
5 Gibson, J .J. (1978) *The Ecological Approach to Visual Perception.* Houghton Mifflin, Boston, MA.
6 Damasio, A. (1999) *The Feeling of What Happens: Body and Emotion in the Making of Consciousness.* William Heinemann, London.
7 Stern, D. (1999) 'Vitality contours: the temporal contour of feelings as the basic unit for constructing the infant's social experience', in P. Rochat (ed.) *Early Social Cognition: Understanding Others in the First Months of Life.* Lawrence Erlbaum, New Jersey.
8 Gendlin, E. (1981) *Focusing.* Bantam Books, New York.
9 Gendlin, E. (1962) *Experiencing and the Creation of Meaning.* North Western University Press, Illinois.
10 Damasio, A. (1996) *Descartes' Error: Emotion, Reason and the Human Brain.* Papermac, London.

11 Neisser, U. (1976) *Cognition and Reality: Principles and Implications of Cognitive Psychology*. W. H. Freeman and Co, New York.
12 Maturana, H. and Varela, F. (1992) *The Tree of Knowledge: The Biological Roots of Human Understanding*, Rev edn. Shambhala, Boston, MA.
13 Hebb, D. O. (1949) *Organisation of Behavior*. Wiley, New York.
14 Merleau-Ponty, M. (1962) *Phenomenology of Perception*, trans. C. Smith. Routledge & Kegan Paul, London.
15 Johnson, M. (1987) *The Body in the Mind: The Bodily Basis of Meaning, Imagination and Reason*. University of Chicago Press, Chicago, IL.
16 Werner, H. and Kaplan, B. (1964) *Symbol Formation: An Organismic-Developmental Approach*. John Wiley & Sons, New York.
17 Bollas, C. (1987) *The Shadow of the Object: Psychoanalysis of the Unthought Known*. Free Association Books, London.

Chapter 3

1 Freud, S. (1976) *Introductory Lectures to Psychoanalysis*, ed. J. Strachey. Penguin Books, London.
2 Husserl, E. (1962) *Ideas: General Introduction to Pure Phenomenology*. Collier Books, New York.
3 Welwood, J. (ed.) (1983) *Awakening the Heart*. Shambhala, Boston, MA.
4 Welwood, J. (1992) *Ordinary Magic: Everyday Life as a Spiritual Path*. Shambhala, Boston, MA.
5 Crook, J. and Fontana, D. (eds) (1990) *Space in Mind: East–West Psychology and Contemporary Buddhism*. Element Books, Dorset, UK.
6 Epstein, M. (1997) *Thoughts Without a Thinker: Psychotherapy from a Buddhist Perspective*. Duckworth, London.
7 Coltart, N. (1992) *Slouching Towards Bethlehem: And Further Psychoanalytic Explorations*. Free Association Books, London.

8 Naranjo, C. and Ornstein, R. (1973) *The Psychology of Meditation*. Penguin Books, London.
9 Rowan, J. (1993) *The Transpersonal: Psychotherapy and Counselling*. Routledge, London.
10 Karamatsu, H. and Hirai, T. (1963) Science of Zazen. *Psychologia*, 6, pp. 86–91.
11 Speeth, K. (1982) On psychotherapeutic attention. *Journal of Transpersonal Psychology*, pp. 141–159.
12 Lesh, T. (1970) Zen meditation and the development of empathy in counsellors. *Journal of Human Psychology*, 10 (1) pp. 39–74.
13 Winnicott, D. W. (1999) *The Maturational Processes and the Facilitating Environment*. Karnac Books, London.
14 North, M. (1975) *Personality Assessment Through Movement*. Plays Inc. Boston, Cambridge University Press.
15 Gibson, J. (1978) *The Ecological Approach to Visual Perception*. Houghton Mifflin, Boston, MA.
16 Bollas, C. (1987) *The Shadow of the Object: Psychoanalysis of the Unthought Known*. Free Association Books, London.
17 Pearsall, P. (1998) *The Heart's Code*. Thorsons, London.

Chapter 4

1 Rajagopalachari, P. (1992) *Love and Death*. SRCM, Denmark.
2 Vivekenanda, Swami (1973) *Raj Yoga: Patanjali's Yoga Aphorisms*. Advaita Ashram, Calcutta, India.
3 Helminski, K. (2000) *The Knowing Heart: A Sufi Path of Transformation*. Shambhala, Boston, MA, and London.
4 Hunt, H. (1995) *On the Nature of Consciousness: Cognitive, Phenomenological and Transpersonal Perspectives*. Yale University Press, New Haven.
5 Johnson, M. (1987) *The Body in the Mind: The Bodily Basis of Meaning, Imagination and Reason*. University of Chicago Press, Chicago, IL.
6 Jung, C. G. (1993) *The Practice of Psychotherapy*. Routledge

    & Kegan Paul, London.
7. Chandra, R. (1989) *Reality at Dawn Vol. 1. Collected Works*. SRCM, Molena, GA.
8. Tart, C. (ed.) (1975) *Yoga Psychology, Haridas Chaudrai Transpersonal Psychology: Perspectives on the Mind from Seven Great Spiritual Traditions*. Harper, San Francisco, CA.
9. Pert, C. (1998) *Molecules of Emotion*. Simon & Schuster, London.
10. Khan, I. (1991) *The Mysticism of Sound and Music*. Element Books, Dorset.
11. Damasio, A. (1999) *The Feeling of What Happens: Body and Emotion in the Making of Consciousness*. William Heinemann, London.
12. Khan, H. I. (1996) *Sufi Teachings: The Smiling Forehead*. East West Publications, London, in association with IHQ of Sufi Movement, Geneva.
13. Bakhtiar, Lalch (1976) *Sufi: Expressions of the Mystic Quest*. Thames and Hudson, London.
14. Attar, Farid Ud-Din (1984) *The Conference of the Birds*, trans. A. Darbandi. Penguin Classics, London.
15. Almaas, A. H. (1998) *Essence with the Elixir of Enlightenment*. Samuel Weiser Inc, York Beach, ME.
16. Pearsall, P. (1998) *The Heart's Code*. Thorsons, London.
17. Damasio, A. (1994) *Descartes' Error: Emotion, Reason and the Human Brain*. Papermac, London.
18. Pearce, C. (1992) *Evolution's End: Claiming the Potential of our Intelligence*. HarperCollins, San Francisco, CA.
19. Lacey, B. (1987) Conversations between heart and brain. *Bulletin, National Institute of Mental Health*, BMB, March 1987.
20. Lynch, J. (1986) *The Language of the Heart*. Basic Books, New York.
21. Stern, D. (1999) 'Vitality contours: the temporal contour of feelings as the basic unit for constructing the infant's social experience', in P. Rochat (ed.) *Early Social Cognition: Understanding Others in the First Months of Life*. Lawrence Erlbaum, New Jersey.

22. Gendlin, E. (1981) *Focusing*. Bantam Books, New York.
23. Merleau-Ponty, M. (1962) *Phenomenology of Perception*, trans. C. Smith. Routledge & Kegan Paul, London.

Chapter 5

1. Khan, I. (1991) *The Mysticism of Sound and Music*. Element Books, Dorset.
2. Kestenberg, J. (1967) *The Role of Movement Patterns in Development*. Dance Notation Bureau, New York.
3. North, M. (1975) *Personality Assessment through Movement*. Plays Inc. Boston, Cambridge University Press.
4. Hawkins, P. and Shohet, R. (1991) *Supervision in the Helping Professions*. Open University Press, Milton Keynes.
5. Berendt, J. E. (1988) *Nada Brahma The World is Sound: Music and the Landscape of Consciousness*. East West Publications, London.
6. Stern, D. (1985) *The Interpersonal World of the Infant*. Basic Books, New York.
7. Geschwind, N. (1965) Disconnection syndromes in animals and man. *Brain*, 88, pp. 237–94, 585–644.
8. Schore, A. (1996) *Affect Regulation and the Origins of Self: The Neurobiology of Emotional Development*. Lawrence Erlbaum, New Jersey.
9. Langer, S. (1979) *Mind: An Essay on Human Feeling*, Vol. 2. Johns Hopkins University Press, Boston, MA.
10. Bohart, A. and Greenberg, L. (eds) (1997) *Empathy Reconsidered: New Directions in Psychotherapy*. American Psychological Association, Washington, DC.
11. Werner, H. and Kaplan, H. (1964) *Symbol Formation: An Organismic-Developmental Approach*. John Wiley & Sons, New York.
12. Kirschenbaum, H. and Henderson, V. (eds) (1990) *The Carl Rogers Reader*. Constable, London.
13. Sewell, L. (1999) *Sight and Sensibility: The Ecopsychology of Perception*. Jeremy Tarcher/Putnam, New York.

Chapter 6

1. Deikman, A. (2001) A functional approach to mysticism. *Journal of Consciousness Studies*, pp. 75–91.
2. Jung, C. (1953–1979) *On Psychological Understanding*. Collected Works, Vol. 3. Routledge & Kegan Paul, London.
3. Lao Tse Tr Gia Fu Feng and English, J. (1972) *Tao Te Ching*. Wildwood, London.
4. Winnicott, D. W. (1999) *The Maturational Processes and the Facilitating Environment*. Karnac Books, London.
5. Gibson, J. (1978) *The Ecological Approach to Visual Perception*. Houghton Mifflin, Boston, MA.
6. Chyta, F. Unpublished thesis.
7. Bakhtiar, Lalch (1976) *Sufi: Expressions of the Mystic Quest*. Thames and Hudson, London.
8. Sheldrake, R. www.sheldrake.org
9. Gendlin, E. (1981) *Focusing*. Bantam Books, New York.

Chapter 7

1. Buber, M. (1937) *I and Thou*, trans. R. G. Smith. T. & T. Clark, Edinburgh.
2. Levin, D. M. (1989) *The Listening Self: Personal Growth, Social Change and the Closure of Metaphysics*. Routledge, London.
3. Klein, N. (2001) Report on Marcos Zapatista non-leader. *Guardian Weekend*, 3 March, p. 14.
4. Gendlin, E. (1981) *Focusing*. Bantam Books, New York.

Conclusion

1. Sheldrake, R. www.sheldrake.org

Further Sources

Sahaj Marg form of Raj Yoga can be contacted on www.srcm.org or write to:

> Liz Kingsnorth
> 38, Temple Village
> Gorebridge
> Midlothian, Scotland EH23 4SQ

The Institute of Heartmath can be contacted on:
> www.heartmath.org
> Institute of Heartmath
> 14700 West Park Ave
> Boulder Creek, CA 95006

Rupert Sheldrake
> www.sheldrake.org

Index

affordances 69, 113, 127
allowing 126
amplification
  of attention 115–18
  of clients' communications 109–11
  and environmental affordance 113
  modalities of listening 9–10, 89, 124–5
  within a therapy session 114–15
  and a yielding environment 111–12
the art(s) 100, 102
attention
  amplifying 116–18
    in rhythmic patterns 115–16
  as forming awareness 66–9
  as environmental affordance 69, 127
  and the heart 82–3
  and perception 57–8
  styles 67, 69
attentional focus 123
  facilitating attunement 104–7
  and psychotherapy practice 60, 62–5
  styles of 70–1
attunement
  affect attunement 23–4, 25, 33, 37, 98

  exploration exercises 107–8
  facilitating attentional focus 104–7
  and influence on feeling 25
  to inner state 25
  and modalities of listening 10, 87, 124
  and narcissistic injury 26–7
  as quality of human contact 88–9
  scope of concept 92–3
  shifts of sensory modality in 24
  in the therapeutic relationship 95–6, 102–4
  v. empathy 100–2
autism 21
autobiographical self 55–6
avoidance culture 128
awareness 66–9

bare attention 61, 62
being, styles of 93–4
biofeedback technology 86
biological processes 42–3
blood pressure 86
bottom–up processing 42, 51, 65, 128
boundedness 74
brain activity 41, 44, 51, 53–4, 84–5

INDEX

brain development 27
Buddhism 60, 69, 77, 87, 107

cardio-energetics 84
carers 16
Cartesian view 13
clients 34–5, 104
cognition 43, 44, 128
coherence 85
common sense 80, 83
connection 36
consciousness 12, 43, 50–5, 109, 123
consultation viii
containment 74
contemplation 59–60, 80

Damasio, Antonio 41, 50–2
dance metaphor 31, 67, 100, 102
depression 129
depth 9–10, 87, 89–90, 120–5
dislocation 74
dissonance 96–7
dynamic patterns 95–6

effort factors 66–7
embodied action 44–5
emotional difficulties 36
emotional narratives 19
emotions 53–4
empathy 100–2
entrainment 17, 86
environment 47, 48
exercises
　amplifying attention 117–18
　deepening and reverberation 124
　exploring attunement 107–8
experience 8–9, 40, 42–3
experiential process 41
experiments in attentional focus 70–1

facial expression 29
feeling 6–7, 8–9, 10, 79, 100
　and attunement to inner state 25
　communication of, and development 21
　and inner vision 129–30
feeling-centred perspective xii–xiv
felt sense 41
flow 31, 67, 68, 95, 96, 101, 109, 116

Gendlin, Eugene 41
Gestalt psychology 5, 120
Gibson, James 47–50

hearkening 119, 123
the heart xii–xiii
the heart
　and attention 82–3
　as centre of being 73–9, 128
　contemporary perspectives on 83–5
　metaphors 75, 76
　as oscillator 85–6
　in philosophy 76–9
　in psychotherapy 82, 125
　relation to feeling and listening 8–10
　as source of intelligence 79–82
heart-centred approach 71–2
heart transplant patients 87
holding 112, 122–4
human contact 3

imagination 45, 80
imitation 15–16
implicit relating 30–1
infant–carer observation 14–16
infant development 4–5, 13, 21–3, 24
inner experience 98
inner space 125

INDEX

insight 32
integrative attitude ix
intelligence 80
intensity 98, 100, 123
intention 10, 18, 90, 122–4
intersubjectivity 12–15, 19–20, 128

knowing 6–7, 53, 56

language 15, 19, 25, 55, 100
learning 22
listening, modalities of 9–10, 86, 87–8, 124
mapping 52–3, 68
matching/mismatching 24, 98
maturation 13, 26
meaning 41, 45–6
meditation xi–xii, 129
   definition and types 61–2
   and psychotherapists 60–1
   and psychotherapy 7–8, 114, 123
meetings 3–4, 6
melody 93–4
memory 22, 55, 80
metaphors *see* dance metaphor, the heart, music metaphor
mimicry 15–16
mindfulness 61
mirroring 98
mismatching 24, 98
moods 32
mother–child bonding 17, 22, 87
   imitation, role of 15–16
   mother's face 21, 27, 29
motion 98–9
motives 20
moulding 93
movement 66, 68, 93, 94, 98
music metaphor 8, 31–2, 104
   chords 96–7
   duet 15
   intensity 100

melody 93–4
sound amplification 109
mystical traditions 126

narcissistic injury 26–7
National Institute of Mental Health 84
neuroscience 41, 44, 50, 51, 82, 84–5, 127
number 98–9

older children, communication with 16–19
openness 64, 123

parallel processing 95–6
perception 6–7
   and attention 57–8
   as guide to action 44–5
   James Gibson's model 47–50, 113
   physiognomic 46–7
   role in therapeutic relationship 57–8
perceptual systems 47, 49
person-centred approach 42
phenomenological approach 42, 60, 69
physiognomic perception 46–7
positive feelings 86
presence 10, 64
professional associations viii
proto-conversations 15
psychotherapists 60–1
psychotherapy
   the art of 11
   and attentional focus 62–5
   change in (Stern) 35–6
   the heart in 82, 125
   ingredients in 126
   and meditation 7–8
   and theory 128
publications x

qualifications vii–viii

rage 128
receptivity 91
relationship 5, 13, 31–2, 40, 65
relaxation 117
resonance 97
response, readiness for 16
reverberation 120, 121, 122, 123, 124
rhythmic patterns 115–16

Sahaj Marg meditation xi, 76
schemas 20, 44, 45
School of Psychotherapy and Counselling (SPC) vii
 publications ix–x
Schore, Allen 26–7
self-organizing systems 44
sense of self 26, 34, 54
 and infant development 4–5
 mapping 52–3
 its origins with others 20–1
 preverbal 28–30
sensorimotor schemas 45
sensory modalities 24–5, 37, 48, 99
sentience *see* feeling
separateness 13
shame 26, 27
shape 98–9
sharing 36, 37
silence 110, 119–20
social beings 19–20
sound 109
space 66, 67, 110
spaciousness 91
spiritual evolution 129
Stern, Daniel
 affect attunement 98
 change in psychotherapy 35–6

infant development 4–5, 24, 28–9, 98–9
Sufic philosophies 77, 80, 81, 92, 105
Sufism 76, 77, 79–82
supervision 95–6
synchronised bioenergetic transmissions 17

Taoism 9, 109
theories 2, 6, 56, 57
therapeutic relationship 22, 27, 41
 amplifying attention in the 114–15
 attunement in the 95–6, 102–4
 clients' perspective 34–5, 104
 perception, role of 57–8
 see also attentional focus
time 66, 98–9
tolerance 83
top–down processing 42, 127
training vii–viii
transitions 24
Trevarthen, Colin 19–20

understanding 32

Varela, Francisco *et al.* 43, 49
verbal communication 86
vitality contours 5, 30, 31, 36, 95–6, 125
vulnerability 63, 64

weight 66, 68
words 46

Yogic philosophies 58, 62, 78, 79, 87

Zen 62, 64, 70